REVOLUTIONIZED PSYCHOLOGY:

PHYSICS OF THE CREATIVE EMERGENT MIND

FRANCES GRACE ROGERS

With the fundamental principles of the Book of Changes, it is possible to arrive at a complete realization of [human's] innate capacities that resemble heaven and earth, that [we] are a microcosm.

I Ching or Book of Changes

Science is not only compatible with spirituality; it is a profound source of spirituality.

Carl Sagan

CONTENTS

Increasing levels of consciousness of the spiritual ascending power within, and how to bring on mental health as well as caring for one's own body, matter that truly matters.

A description of encounters with the pathological field of psychology. Toward the end of the Chapter is a description of Zeitgeist Moving Forward, a 2011 documentary which validates that pathology as well as recommending changes in order to fulfill human needs.

A brief description of the wondrous result of 28 years of achievement and ongoing evolution of consciousness.

Music by Frances Grace Rogers is available on soundcloud.com/the-emergent-mind

CHAPTER ONE

AN EXTENDED INTRODUCTION

The purpose of this book is to share knowledge achieved through 28 years of research, introspection, and countless insights, which have changed my life. I have become fully aware of the value of wisdom: "the ability to discern or judge what is true, right, or lasting, insight."[1] Wisdom is also intertwined with spirituality and humane values: honesty/sincerity, justice/fairness, and compassion/kindness. Wisdom can bring positive change to humanity; it also supports fulfillment of human needs.

There are numerous great men in humanity's history whose lives and mental achievements serve as an example of wisdom and the physics of the mind. While no one is born wise, it can be achieved over time through experience, knowledge, intelligence, and ongoing evolution of consciousness, which actually changes the functioning of the sequential and spatial hemispheres of the phenomenal human brain. Those great men, like most people, are born with the innate capacity for wholeness, balance, and self-actualization—the bringing to actual one's whole self—united by the human spirit that exists in all people.

Essentially this writing is a top-down view, for it is encouraging to know the potential wisdom for humanity. That positive knowledge provides awareness of the countless unbalanced people who have imposed impediments to wholeness by human constructionism in order to gain control over others. Those impediments are accomplished by oppressing what is true, right, and good. Oppression in any form is destructive. Destructive evil is not the opposite of good but the destroyer of the good. That oppression is primarily of the spatial hemisphere's capacity for higher levels of functioning. Essentially, they are rendered unconscious.

The man of wisdom who provides knowledge of the physics of the mind is Nobel laureate, neuropsychologist, neurobiologist Roger Wolcott Sperry, which gives credence to ancient sages' wisdom. *Sage* is an old term used for a profoundly wise person who is practical, intuitive, and insightful, gaining wisdom through experience and self-reflection. Self-reflection is "the capacity of humans to exercise introspection and the willingness to learn more about their fundamental nature, purpose, and essence."[2]

Sages are distinguished from the exploitative nature of gurus or the sorcerous traits of shamans. True sages are Humanists who believe in humanity's potential to make positive changes as well as the wisdom of nature. Ancient sages in China developed the *I Ching*, a book of wisdom, which began as a book of poetry. It is the only book of its kind, for it uses metaphors of nature regarding the creative spatial right hemisphere and the receptive sequential left hemisphere of the human brain.

A modern sage was physicist Stephen Hawking whose accomplishments exposed the basis for the laws of nature as well as a sense of purpose. He, like Albert Einstein and Roger Wolcott Sperry, also exposed many of the impediments imposed by human constructionism, including human myth.

Roger Sperry was fully aware that the system of psychology needs to be revolutionized, especially lack of consciousness of the true nature of mind and psyche:

> "This is the general stance of modern behavioral science out of which comes today's prevailing objective, mechanistic, materialistic, behavioristic, fatalistic, reductionist view of the nature of mind and psyche. This kind of thinking is not confined to our laboratories and the classrooms, of course. It leaks and spreads, and though never officially imposed on the societies of the Western world, we nevertheless see the pervasive influence of creeping materialism everywhere we turn."[3]

My previous book, *Wholistic Psychology: To Revolutionize the Mindset Supporting the Trumpism of Materialistic Society,* 2017, foreshadowed by my book, *Empowered Humans: The Phenomenon of Being,* 2016, included the work of Stephen Hawking, Roger Wolcott Sperry, and others with whole minds. However, its focus was more on the conservative left brain dominance, which resists change, over spatial right brain tendency toward liberalism, which advocates positive change for humanity. That dominance of left brain functioning is obvious in the election of Donald Trump as President of the United States, which invoked the consideration to expand the contents of my previous writings. I realized that conservatives who hold to traditional attitudes and values, typically in relation to politics, religion, and even the pathological field of psychology, are responsible for the big divide between the left and right hemispheres of the brain.

That book became a necessity after an encounter with the psychology department at Rollins College, in Winter Park, Florida, where I achieved my BS degree in Psychology. I protested, in writing, the announced course at the 2017 Alumni meeting, "The Right Brain/Left Brain Myth," which served to confirm that the field of psychology continues to contribute to our unbalanced human world, as well as the numerous unbalanced people working in the field.

The written response received was proof that psychology contains no valid science. That letter, as well, confirmed the fact that it is complacency which maintains that lack of balance. Complacency is defined as "self-satisfaction, especially when accompanied by unawareness of actual dangers or deficiencies."[4]

The source of encouragement, though, was Betty Edwards, author of *Drawing on the Right Side the Brain,*[5] who expressed her thoughts regarding my previous achievements, "Happy to know that a strong advocate is working hard to put things right. Many people these days are denying the work of Sperry and others, and we see all around us the triumph of the left brain. But there are others, like you and perhaps myself, who are knocking at the foundations and will eventually be heard."

Ongoing insights have aroused awareness that the uniqueness of each individual is reflective of the intertwining of all aspects of the multiple dimension human as well as the countless dimensions of each individual's environment, including relationships. *The Interpersonal Theory of Psychology,*[6] by Psychiatrist Harry Stack Sullivan, focuses on oppressive human relationships as the source of mental dysfunction.

It is also evidenced in the achievements of another man of wisdom, Humanist Psychologist Abraham Harold Maslow, who exposes humanity's social needs in his hierarchy of human needs. Lack of fulfillment of those needs can prevent self-actualization, which he considered to be the highest of human callings. His ongoing mental accomplishments are also basic to revolutionizing psychology.

Stephen Jay Gould, paleontologist, evolutionary biologist, and historian of science, authored ten books regarding his significant findings. His book, *The Mismeasure of Man*[7], is also a major contribution to the revolution of psychology. Gould considers wisdom to be an ideal achievement.

The accomplishments of the referenced men in this Chapter were not addressed in my education, even my MS degree in Clinical Psychology achieved at the University of Central Florida in Orlando. During the many years working as a mental health counsellor in Maitland, Florida, I became fully aware of the pathological psychology included in my education. During those years, I learned from my clients about many of the impediments to mental health, especially abuse and oppression. That learning was validated when I found Psychiatrist Thomas S. Szasz's book, *The Myth of Mental Illness.*[8]

Those years of learning contributed to the awakening of my higher spatial brain's capabilities by a vision that occurred on August 6, 1991, the 48th anniversary of my birth. That awakening was preceded by strange and disturbing visual dreams that began January, 1990. Those dreams became verbal when poetry began to pour from my mind on April 1, 1990. Some of those poems included events occurring to my clients.

While Psychiatrist Henri F. Ellenberger considers that poetry to be a creative illness,[9] it is not an illness at all, for my dreaming foreshadowed my awakening, which also exposed many of the illusions of my life. That transforming event impelled me to begin research to find out what was happening to my mind. It was truly serendipitous to discover Roger Wolcott Sperry in Betty Edwards' book, Chapter 3, *Your Brain, The Right and Left of it* in 1995. I read that book after art began to be evoked by my creative spatial hemisphere. My first musical composition had occurred two years earlier at age 50.

Further achievements by Sperry were found in 2015, which required corrections to knowledge exposed in previous writings. His achievements overcame some of the idiocy which I had found in Leonard Shlain's book, *Art & Physics: Parallel Visions in Space, Time, & Light,*[10] especially the invalid physics theory of parallel universes, which is otherworldly, and paranormal precognition.

The intertwining of countless insights on what is true and right, as well as finding many more insightful men substantiating and furthering Sperry's knowledge, resulted in my 4th book, published in 2016, *Empowered Humans: The Phenomenon of Being,* regarding the human capacity for wholeness and balance. It included knowledge, shared by personal example, especially the process of overcoming the man-made impediments to wholeness, as well as fulfilling my creative spatial brain talents of musical compositions and art, which was included in the book to elaborate the symbolism in my paintings.

Essentially it seemed to be the culmination of my enlightenment, including the wisdom of nature.

That book also made me fully aware of the effect of personal and societal history of any theorist's psychological theory. It was also obvious in psychological theorist Carl Jung's statement, "Philosophical criticism has helped me to see that every psychology— my own included—has the character of a subjective confession . . . Even when I am dealing with empirical data I am necessarily speaking about myself."[11] I also became aware that comparing that writing to my first book, *Of Golden Frogs and Such: A Story of Survival and Transformation*, 2006, would be like comparing a rotary telephone with an iPhone X. Yet every writing was necessary in order to gradually overcome obstructions of consciousness and achieving more self-knowledge.

With continual evolution of consciousness, I have become cognizant of the fact that I had been whole for most of life due to my fascination with nature and music, even as a child. I believed that my previous book, *Wholistic Psychology: To Revolutionize the Mindset Supporting the Trumpism of Materialistic Society,* was my final writing. Included in that writing was the discovery of another amazing man, Gottfried Wilhelm Leibniz, a 17th century philosopher and mathematician.

According to contributors to Wikipedia, "Leibniz made major contributions to physics and technology, and anticipated notions that surfaced much later in philosophy, probability theory, biology, medicine, geology, psychology, linguistics, and computer science. He wrote works on philosophy, politics, law, ethics, theology, history, and philology [language studies]. Leibniz's contributions to this vast array of subjects were scattered in various learned journals, in tens of thousands of letters, and in unpublished manuscripts. He wrote in several languages, but primarily in Latin, French, and German. There is no complete gathering of the writings of Leibniz in English."

"Leibniz's work had a great impact on the field of psychology. Leibniz thought that there are many small perceptions of which we perceive but of which we are unaware. He believed that by the principle that phenomena found in nature were continuous by default, it was likely that the transition between conscious and unconscious states had intermediary steps. For this to be true, there must also be a portion of the mind of which we are unaware at any given time. His theory regarding consciousness in relation to the principle of continuity can be seen as an early theory regarding stages of sleep. In this way, Leibniz's theory of perception can be viewed as one of many theories leading up to the idea of the unconscious."[12]

Leibniz's phenomenal mental achievements are reflective of both sequential and spatial brain functioning, for he is obviously aware of the intertwining of all subjects.

After the publication of *Wholistic Psychology* in 2017, I started a new project. I began to orchestrate many of my previous piano compositions to fulfill a desire to create my first Concerto. I then realized that some of those compositions fit together. Over time and frequently listening to my recorded movements to make corrections, I was astonished to realize that my music was essentially a self-fulfilling prophecy: "a prediction that directly or indirectly causes itself to become true, by the very terms of the prophecy itself, due to positive feedback between belief and behavior.[13] My music was created by my spatial and sequential hemispheres, including subconscious beliefs.

It is a scaled up version of Wholistic Psychology and predicted many of my discoveries, as well as this writing.

That insight was a major source of a realization of the intertwining of all aspects of the multidimensional human, essentially a scaled down version of Leibniz's intertwining of all of society's subjects. In a sense, it gives credence to James Gleick's *Chaos; Making a New Science.*[14] That science is revolutionary, essentially unifying many sciences. Those Chaos scientists became aware of patterns in nature that appeared on different scales at the same time. I became aware that their capacity to discern patterns is intuition, and that scaling systems is a concept that also applies to individuals, including the human body, as well as society. Those Chaos scientists' work was derided by many in the scientific community. Glieck's assessment is one that is agreeable to explain that derision: "Shallow ideas can be assimilated; ideas that require people to reorganize their picture of the world provoke hostility."

* * *

I have finally achieved a state of joy which goes far beyond hedonistic happiness—the pleasures of the five senses; that state of joy had been evidenced in some great men, including the ancient Chinese sages. It was expressed in my 7th composition titled *The Joy of Freedom, Insight, and Harmony.* That composition also includes more evidence why Ludwig Van Beethoven's 9th Symphony was my favorite, for his last movement is a chorale rendition of *Ode to Joy,* a poem by Friedrich Schiller that he had been planning to put to music for 30 years. He had verbally altered that poem to fit with his insights.

My 7th composition includes a melodic rendition of *A Psalm of Wisdom,* Appendix I, which is a revolutionized version of Henry Wadsworth Longfellow's *Psalm of Life*, discovered when I was a teenager. That poem remained in my subconscious mind and influenced many of my insights, my poetry, as well as an initial piano composition titled *A Psalm of Life.*

My Concerto is available on soundcloud.com/the-emergent-mind. As said on that website, I perform the music via Reason. It is a computer music program which connects with an electric keyboard. Each instrument is recorded separately.

Unfortunately, it is rare for women's classical compositions to be played by an orchestra. In 2000 I met a music professor at Florida State University who rejected me, a previous orchestrated composition I shared with him, as well as a new composition, *Embrace the Mystery,* for which I had desired feedback. I later found out that a young female student at FSU, who wanted to focus on music composition rather than performance, was also rejected by that man.

CHAPTER TWO

THE HUMAN REFLECTION OF NATURE

I became an admirer of Stephen Hawking many years ago after reading his book, *A Brief History of Time: From the Big Bang to Black Holes,*[15] the result of findings as a theoretical physicist, cosmologist, and teacher. He has become famous for his TV shows offering knowledge to humanity. While his biography is offered in many ways, none are as pertinent as his telling his own story in the 2013 Documentary, *Hawking.* It is a film which reflects his introspection and attaining wholeness. Fortunate to have been raised in a nurturing environment, he became a lover of life in his youth. Encouraged to become a medical professional, like his father, Hawking believes that he was fortunate to have chosen to pursue his interest in physics, a field in which he could continue to function with a horrendous physical disability. I believe his spatial brain did the choosing—the inner body awareness that something was amiss.

Hawking was diagnosed with ALS disease at age twenty with expectation of only a few years of life. Through love for his wife and through Wilhelm Richard Wagner's music, he coped with his illness and remarkably lived another 56 years.

In a 2012 mini-series documentary, *Stephen Hawking's Grand Design,* Hawking introduced himself as a "physicist, cosmologist, and something of a dreamer. Although I cannot move and have to speak through a computer, in my mind, I am free." Stephen Hawking was definitely a dreamer, which contributed to his countless insights into the functions of nature. His mind freedom was from any human constructionism—more in balance with the harmony of nature.

Hawking's introduction was exactly the same in the 2011 documentary, *Did God Create the Universe?* The answer he finds is consistent with Einstein's statements regarding that insane personification of nature's energy:

> "I cannot imagine a God who rewards and punishes the objects of his creation, whose purposes are modeled after our own—a God, in short, who is but a reflection of human frailty. Neither can I believe that the individual survives the death of his body, although feeble souls harbor such thoughts through fear or ridiculous egotism."[16]

Hawking's findings also provided relief, evidenced in his words: "For centuries it was believed that disabled people like me were living under a curse inflicted by god. Well I suppose it's possible that I have upset someone up there, I prefer to believe it can be explained another way, by the laws of nature." His statement is confirmed by this author's knowledge that this world is both accidental and orderly; the sun shines on everyone, not a chosen few; tragic events occur to both good and bad people.

The content of Hawking's two documentaries is inextricably intertwined, each coming from a different direction. In the *Grand Design* he takes us back, scientifically, to the very beginning when there was only negative space and energy, the contraction before the big bang. He leads us through the multidimensional process of change resulting in the formation of planet earth by the fixed laws of nature. He takes us to the very rudiments of life that operates on every scale in string theory.

Hawking also addresses a major existential question, "Is there a meaning to life?" His conclusion is that life has the meaning we give it. That answer is compatible with my insight—the freedom to be. Much more knowledge is presented by Hawking, all thick with meaning. He did, indeed, delve into the depth of life and its meaning, qualifying him as a sage. In a sense, Stephen Hawking, like Albert Einstein, is immortal due to knowledge that can affect human understanding of the laws of nature until the end of time.

Another significant aspect of the *Grand Design* is Hawking's likening that creative energy to music, not just any music but the sound of vibrating strings. It is the same kind of music that positively affects the human fetus in the womb and promotes growth in plants; in contrast, hard rock music actually destroys plants.

Hawking perceives everything as physics—the immutable laws—producing the amazing harmonious orchestration of nature. Roger Wolcott Sperry, like Hawking, was aware of the creative forces existing in nature, as well as in humans; he said "The creative forces and creativity itself becomes intricately interfused." Einstein was also aware of human creativity, associated with nature. He learned to play violin as a boy; over the years he came to believe that Wolfgang

Amadeus Mozart's music reflected the harmony of nature. Classical music is, indeed, physics, as well as a universal language.

In the *Grand Design* Hawking also states that our earth is just right for us and quotes Carl Sagan, renowned astronomer, cosmologist, astrophysicist, and author, "We are a way for the universe to know itself." Similar is Leonardo da Vinci's assertion in the 15th century: to know the workings of the human is to know the workings of the universe.[17] Ancient sages knew, as well, that humans have innate capacities resembling heaven and earth—a microcosm.

It is a concept which gives credence to my discovery of the multi-dimensional reflective human, the basis for Revolutionized Psychology:

> Not only are we capable of self-reflection, but humans are a reflection of nature. We are comprised of our dual brains, our bodies, and the physical energy to function. We have evolved to reflect, and to reflect on the world around us in our spatial capabilities, where time is irrelevant; and in our timely sequential processes—including the past, present, and anticipation of the future. We also have evolved to reflect the world in our bodies consisting of the many properties of biology and physics: chemistry, mechanics of movement, proportion, including the Golden ratio of pi, and genes that determine form. That physiological energy is evidenced in behavior.
>
> Space-time-matter-energy, as in nature, forms a continuum, an essential word in its established

meaning: "a continuous extent, succession, or whole, no part of which can be distinguished from neighboring parts except by arbitrary division."[18] Those arbitrary divisions abound in man-made constructs, especially in shamanism, religion, and the belief based field of psychology.

That which serves to unify the multidimensional human is the human spirit—the animating life force—our fifth dimension and the greatest mystery of all. That energy is ubiquitous and exists on every level of life, from the microcosm to the macrocosm. It has provoked a sense of wonder throughout recorded history to those conscious enough to perceive it. It is likely to have evoked Albert Einstein's words, "A knowledge of the existence of something we cannot penetrate, of the manifestations of the profoundest reason and the most radiant beauty—it is this knowledge and this emotion that constitute the truly religious attitude; in this sense, and in this alone, I am a deeply religious man."[19] Hawking extended that concept when he said that the same spirit exists in everyone.

Ancient sages revered that energy as the Divine One: "To know this One means to know oneself in relation to the cosmic forces, for this One is the ascending force of life in nature and in man."[20]

Albert Einstein's wisdom is evident in his numerous writings and wise quotes regarding what is true, right, and good. He was also a critic of capitalism, which is materialistic, and strongly favored socialist policies that are egalitarian, as well as democracy. In a sense he predicted what is currently happening due to the election of psychopath Donald Trump, which has increased oppression and lack of human rights.

Albert Schweitzer, medical doctor, theologian, philosopher, and musician, like Einstein, encountered that spiritual energy within. Disturbed by what he considered to be the collapse of civilization in early 20th century Europe—the lack of ethics or humanitarian ideals—he ruminated extensively on the question, "What is civilization?" He found no satisfactory answer in religion or philosophy and believed he was in practically unexplored land.

Schweitzer describes an awakening experience while on a boat trip in Africa: The iron door yielded. There flashed upon my mind, unforeseen and unsought, the phrase, Ehrfurcht vor dem Leben—to be in awe of the mystery of life. Schweitzer's phrase has also been interpreted as reverence for life. [21]

The human spirit is expressed in numerous ways, especially reverence for life and fortitude—the "strength of mind that enables a person to encounter danger or bear pain or adversity with courage."[22] Stephen Hawking exhibited the spiritual in his fortitude, the amazing strength to cope with his illness, as well as reverence for life—to use whatever time he had to fulfill his potential.

I began a journal in January, 1990 when strange and disturbing dreams occurred. My ongoing journaling included the vision on August 6, 1991, the event of my awakening.

> "I saw a light that began to move and flow in every possible soft color, in dimensions that even defy imagination and certainly any concept I have of space, of direction, of size, or shape. In that vision,

the structure of the [humanly constructed] room totally dissipated as did its contents, as though carried by that light; everything seemed to be turning inside out and upside down from what it was and absolutely topsy-turvy to anything rational."

That turning, inside out and upside down, is a form known to exist in physics' string theory. It was, for me, a vision of the spiritual energy in my soul. The words produced by that experience: I can see everything! The elation of my awakening—instantaneous shift in consciousness—dissipated as that *seeing* moved through multiple dimensions, and the illusions of my life began to topple. The first was a change in visual perception, particularly of size. The next was when, in my mind, I saw images of history moving like a film running at high speed—the destruction done in the name of God. Those moving scenes produced a sudden insight: I had not ever been in control of anything, including my own mind.

* * *

As said in the first chapter, another man of wisdom who provides knowledge of the physics of the mind is Nobel laureate, neuropsychologist, neurobiologist Roger Wolcott Sperry, which gives credence to ancient sages' wisdom, as well as other self-actualized people. He was also totally aware of the need to revolutionize shallow, spiritless, belief based psychology supportive of a materialistic society.

Sperry, together with two colleagues, received the 1981 Nobel Prize in Physiology and Medicine for divided brain experiments. Those experiments were done with people whose corpus callosum, the thick band of nerve fibers connecting the two hemispheres, had been surgically severed to control severe epileptic seizures. Those studies resulted in conclusive evidence of the lateralization of the human brain: the right hemisphere controls the left side of the body, and the left hemisphere controls the right side of the body.

That work was only one dimension of his discoveries, for he was interested in everything from the cosmos to the finite workings of the amazing human brain. That interest began in childhood; he spent his early years on a farm where he developed a lifelong interest in nature. Theodore J. Voneida, a neurobiology educator, both colleague and friend of Sperry, offers Sperry's biology, including his accomplishments, in *A Biographical Memoir.* He concludes that biography with, "Scientist, teacher, philosopher, humanist—Roger Sperry has left us a rich legacy of ideas and a challenge to foster the emergence of new understandings of human capabilities and responsibilities." [23]

It is evident that Sperry, too, was a creative, wise, whole, and balanced man. According to Voneida: "Sperry was a quiet, thoughtful, and modest man with an insatiable curiosity. He never stopped working, questioning, or learning up until his death in 1994 of ALS or Lou Gehrig's disease. You could often find Sperry in his office with his feet propped up on his desk scribbling in his notebook or deep in thought. Sperry was an avid paleontologist and displayed his large fossil collection in his home. He was also a very talented sculptor, artist, and ceramicist." [24]

Over time and continued research, Sperry knew that the left brain is superior in analytical, sequential, and linguistics; the right brain performs better in holistic, parallel, and spatial abilities. His comprehension evolved to conclude that the brain is:

> "Indeed a conscious system in its own right, perceiving, thinking, remembering, reasoning, willing, and emoting, all at a characteristically human level…, both the left and the right hemisphere may be conscious simultaneously in different, even in mutually conflicting, mental experiences that run along in parallel."

He also reports that "The split brain behaves in many respects like two separate brains, providing new research possibilities."

Those mutually conflicting mental experiences, referred to by Sperry, are indicative of the unconscious, the spatial brain knowledge which has been oppressed. Sperry's work also gives credence to instincts hard-wired in the brain as well as the discovery of neuroplasticity. It was once believed the human brain is fully developed by age six; later, that development was extended to age ten. Now it is known that the brain can change throughout life through multidimensional experiences. Current research reveals that experience actually changes the brain's physical structure and functional organization.[25] Yet not all neuroscience is valid, like those who are the source of controversy over right and left brain functioning. They base their conclusions on electronic imaging of neuron activity, denying the fact of suppression of spatial brain knowledge—the unconscious.

Sperry's work continued to progress. In *Holding Course Amid Shifting Paradigms,* Sperry proposes a shift from scientific materialism to mentalism; a shift from the reductionism of the human to the atomic level to comprehending that the whole is more than the sum of its parts. His new model "involves an added emphasis on the space-time or pattern factors in causation as opposed to the material, physical factors."[26]

In physics, space-time is an additional continuum, which opens the door to numerous dimensions. The mentalism of which Sperry speaks also explains many mysteries, including synchronicity, which simply means to be in sync with the spirit of another living entity. Theodore J. Voneida provides an informed summation regarding Sperry's work within that arena:

> The concept of emergence, according to Sperry, "occurs whenever the interaction between 2 or more entities, be they sub particles, atoms or molecules, creates a new entity with new laws and properties formerly nonexistent in the universe." He notes the parallel with quantum physics in which "interactions among subatomic particles result in emergent properties which in no way resemble the particles from which they arose."
>
> Thus, consciousness, in Sperry's view, while generated by and dependent on neural activity, is nonetheless separate from it. Consciousness

emerges from the activity of cerebral networks as an independent entity. This newly emerged property which we call "mind" or "consciousness," continually feeds back to the central nervous system, resulting in a highly dynamic process of emergence, feedback (downward causation), newly emergent states, further feedback, and so forth. Reducing consciousness to its separate components obliterates the emergent phenomenon of "mind" with all its great power and uniqueness.[27]

Sperry's emergent mind is the process of evolving consciousness. In *Holding Course Amid Shifting Paradigms* Sperry quotes himself from previous articles:

"Our new acceptance in science of consciousness and subjectivity, the mental and cognitive, or spiritual does not—as frequently inferred—open the door of science to the supernatural, the mystical, the paranormal, the occult, otherworldly—nor, in short, to any form of unembodied mind or spirit. The strength and promise of the new macro mental outlook is in just the opposite, that is, in taking our ultimate guideline beliefs, and resultant social values out of the realm of the supernatural and otherworldly uncertainties and grounding them in a more realistic realm of knowledge and truth, consistent with science and empiric verification."

He continued by elevating his concepts from the individual to the global level, stating that:

> "The new paradigm affirms that the world we live in is driven not solely by mindless physical forces but, more crucially, by subjective human values. Human values become the underlying key to world change."

Those subjective human values are the source of human constructionism, including religion. Like Einstein said, that subjectivity can be human depravity, fear, or ridiculous egotism. Positive world change definitely will occur when those values become humane, emanated by the higher spatial brain's abilities.

Sperry also wrote an article titled *Mind, Brain, and Humanist Values.*[28] In that article Sperry expressed his opposition to mental science that omitted humane values. Essentially, that so-called science is not science at all.

The conclusion of Sperry's *Holding Course Amid Shifting Paradigms* was as follows:

> "Humanity's creator thus becomes the vast interwoven fabric of all evolving nature. The creative forces and creation itself become inextricably interfused, making it immoral, even sacrilegious, to degrade earthly existence or to treat it merely as a way station."

Sperry's multidimensional concepts are congruent with the wisdom of the ancient sages, as well as Stephen Hawking and Albert Einstein who were aware of the wisdom of nature.

Those ancient Chinese sages were cognizant of the spatial and sequential hemispheres of the human brain. The spatial brain, called the Creative Yang force, associated with heaven—the cosmos— and the sequential brain, the Receptive Yin force, associated with the earth, constitute the primary forms of the six line hexagrams throughout the book. Being fully receptive to the higher spatial brain's knowledge is a major value addressed in the hexagram *Modesty*, #15, in which there is nothing extreme. Extremity, in any form, does not further balance; it frequently brings on arrogance. The balance between the two modes of functioning is addressed in the hexagram of *Peace*, #11. It is in a commentary regarding that hexagram that the dual hemispheres are addressed, "… the movement of yang is thought of as being toward the right and that of yin toward the left."[29] Most of the comments in the *I Ching* were by Confucius or his disciples. Confucius knew it was a book of wisdom.

* * *

As Hawking, Einstein, and Sperry knew, one of the major impediments to wholeness is mythological religious beliefs. They validated one of my April, 1990 poems:

In my dream appeared a being,
fascinating concept and unique,
filled with light, yet fully human.

No extremes of good or bad,
not for worship or for hate.

Time has come for destruction
of defiled being, the split healed.
Master plan, conceived by man,
double-binds the mind, and
futility darkens the Spirit.

A major word in that poem is futility, which is a lack of a sense of self-worth. It has been happening to women for over 5000 years, since patriarchal religion was invented by Moses in the old testament of the bible. He was raised as an Egyptian prince in a Pharaoh's harem where women were essentially treated as sex slaves to fulfill the animalistic instinct to reproduce one's genes in another generation. The only father he knew was the ruling Pharaoh who, like previous Pharaohs, conceived himself as a god. In Moses' book of Genesis, women were created as a second sex by a jealous god, strikingly similar to his Pharaoh father, particularly jealous of women's capacity to give birth. Facing the truth of evil was also forbidden, which substantiates complacency. Patriarchy and religion continue to be inextricably intertwined.

There are many others who know the truth of that evil like Thomas Paine, an 18th century writer, political activist, philosopher, and revolutionary; he said, "Whenever we read the obscene stories, the voluptuous debaucheries, the cruel and tortuous executions, the unrelenting vindictiveness with which more than half the Bible is filled, it would be more consistent that we call it the word of a demon than the word of God. It is a history of wickedness that has served to corrupt and brutalize mankind."[30]

Nobel Laureate Bertrand Russell, another philosopher who believed in freedom of thought and humanitarian ideals, maintained that religion, despite any positive effects it may have, "serves to impede knowledge, foster fear and dependency, and is responsible for much of the war, oppression, and misery of the world."[31]

In contrast, there was a Golden Age in Egypt 10,000 years ago; the contralateral right and left brain's arrangement was evidenced in hieroglyphical writings. Women were considered equal to men; there was even a female pharaoh before the transition to patriarchy by so-called spiritual Egyptians. It is obvious that shift was to overcome the creativity of Mother Nature, which had been addressed in Greek writings.

There was also a Golden Age in China, which was achieved by the Shang dynasty in the Yellow River Valley—the cradle of Chinese civilization—during the second millennium BCE. Women, during that period, enjoyed a higher and better status than in any other time of China's history. Toward the end of the Shang Dynasty, the *I Ching* was conceived by a group of sages.

That Golden Age in China ended though, for patriarchy crept in from the West. According to Pedro Ccinos Arcones, "….it came with people speaking Indo-European languages and was reflected in the influence on the Zhou Kings that defeated the Shang Dynasty and started the oppression of women in China." [32]

Those new Zhou Kings altered the *I Ching* by adding hexagrams 31-64, imposed with layers of patriarchal interpretations. The Spatial Creative Yang force was redefined as masculine and the Sequential

Yin force as feminine, placing women in the submissive role beneath the powerful male. Those patriarchal Chinese leaders made sex slaves, called concubines, an institutional part of that culture.

One of the most popular Western interpretations is Richard Wilhelm's *I Ching or Book of Changes.* His first 1924 publication was in German. Carl Baynes' initial English translation *was* published in 1950 and republished many times since then. A more recent rendition is by Taoist Master Alfred Juang, *The Complete I Ching.*[33] Both books are not only contaminated by patriarchy but by their author's subjectivity. That contamination is obvious when comparing what Juang claims to be the original poems, which he includes in his book, with his interpretations. He is fully enmeshed in the traditions of the Zhou Dynasty.

Richard Wilhelm's use of the word *god* for the spirit is also an example. That word, with all its implications, does not exist in those supposedly original poems. Wilhelm's belief in Christianity is evident when he footnotes biblical references to Jesus, distorting the original concepts to fit with his beliefs.

I discovered Wilhelm's interpretation in 1994. I found it worth the effort to see through that subjectivity, not only to discern the wisdom achieved by the left and right hemispheres, but it also includes humane values: honesty and sincerity, compassion/kindness, justice/fairness, and wisdom. Various hexagrams substantiated many of my poems, especially regarding the human spirit.

* * *

The result of that Golden Age in Egypt remained in the sub-culture of Egypt, as evidenced in the 1945 discovery of the Nag Hammadi Library in southern Egypt and its subsequent translation, completed in the '70s. It has revealed a very different history and story than those recorded in the New Testament of the Christian Bible. The response of the Church to that discovery has generally been one of discounting those writings as heretical. Even the word, *Gnostic*, a derivative of *gnosis*—the Greek noun for knowledge—has been demonized.

Marvin Meyer is regarded as a foremost scholar of Gnosticism, and his expertise is enlightening to many, particularly in his book, *The Gnostic Gospels of Jesus*.[34] Regarding Gnosticism in general, Meyer says: "In Gnostic texts, unlike gospels of the cross [the four gospels in the New Testament], knowledge is more important than faith, and knowledge of oneself leads to salvation." Definitely reflective of the wisdom of introspection—the pathway to self-knowledge and healing the wounds of one's past.

Meyer's analysis of the Gnostic book of the Great Invisible Spirit and Secret Book of John results in his thought that the unfolding of the divine One is as much a story about psychology as it is about mythology and metaphysics: "the expressions of the divine One are mental capabilities—mind (nous), forethought (pronoia), thought (enoia), insight (epinoia), wisdom (sophia), even mindlessness (aponoia)."

It is remarkable that the term *Divine One* is the one used by those ancient Chinese sages, as well as the attributes of both spatial and sequential brain functioning. *Mind,* of course, includes both brains. Forethought is the capacity to plan ahead; thought can be multidimensional. Insight is a dual brain phenomenon, and wisdom, gained through introspection and experience, is that which moves us forward and stands the test of time—lasting. Mindlessness is the absence of thinking and lack of consciousness.

Meyer tells us that *The Gospel of Thomas* is different from other Gnostic writings, for Jesus is portrayed as imparting wisdom in dialogue. In that gospel there is no mention of physical miracles, fulfilling prophecy, apocalyptic warning, nor does Jesus place himself above those around him except as an example.

The similarities between the hidden sayings of Jesus in Marvin Meyer's translation of *The Gospel of Thomas* with Flatland/Spaceland concepts, described in Chapter Three, as well as the *I Ching*, were just as surprising as the Divine One—that ascending force in nature and humans. Even though he had that ridiculous belief in the father god, the following statements by Jesus are significant:

"Let one who seeks not stop seeking until one finds; when one finds, one will be troubled; when one is troubled, one will marvel and reign over all." (2:1-4) *One will be troubled* is similar to my initial encounter with my higher spatial brain capabilities. Comparable is the concept, "Difficulty in the Beginning," in the Book of Changes, when a major shift in consciousness occurs. Then, of course, the marvel that comes with enlightenment—"I can see everything."

Jesus continues with: "If your leaders say to you, 'Look, the kingdom is in heaven,' then the birds of heaven will precede you. If they say to you 'It is in the sea,' then the fish will precede you. Rather, the kingdom is inside you and it is outside you." (3: 1-3).

"Know what is in front of your face, and what is hidden from you will be disclosed to you." (5: 1) This speaks of the unified brain's capacity to see and hear without the distortion of subjectivity, enmeshment, or the fog of prejudice, which opens the door to countless revelations.

"When you make the two into one, you will become children of humankind." (106) What "the two" refers to is answered in Jesus' response to a question posed to him regarding entering the kingdom of heaven: "When you make eyes in place of an eye, a hand in place of a hand, a foot in place of a foot, an image in place of an image, then you will enter." (22) To use both eyes and experience that contra-lateral arrangement is obvious. It can be likened to Confucius' commentary referring to heaven (creative yang force) and earth (timely yin force) as being inside each of us. That commentary suggests Confucius, or one of his disciples, knew the truth of our dual brains.

Closely related and supportive of the synthesis of both spatial and sequential capabilities is another maxim by Jesus: "... I say if one is whole, one will be filled with light, but if one is divided, one will be filled with darkness." (61: 5) Jesus acknowledges intuition as a blessing; he makes numerous references to self-examination.

As to the creative potential, Jesus' knowledge is reflected in his words: "Do not let your right hand know what your left hand is doing." (62: 2) He is prohibiting that egoistic tendency to filter out spatial brain capabilities that threaten one's beliefs, and/or to interpret any experience through the fog of prejudice or dogma.

Jesus, as portrayed by Thomas, was opposed to dogma that closes the door to new knowledge and gave few commandments. In addition to the one regarding creativity, he said, "Do not lie." (6: 2) and "Be on guard against the world." (21: 6) It is the necessity of setting boundaries on oneself as well as others.

In response to the question, "When will the kingdom come?" Jesus said, "It will not come by watching for it. It will not be said 'Look, here it is,' or 'Look, there it is.' Rather, the father's kingdom is spread out upon the earth, and people do not see it." (113: 3, 4)

Roger Wolcott Sperry was also fully aware of the celestial region of the mind. In a sense it is the heaven within as well as in nature. Even though the Gnostic Gospels have been discounted, as well as the distortion of the work of those Chinese sages, Sperry, through valid science, has provided knowledge of the two hemispheres of the human brain and psyche [the human soul, mind, and spirit]. He has, indeed, left a rich legacy for humanity.

* * * *

The first movement of my Concerto, titled *Our Connection with Nature, and The Greatest Mystery of all*, foreshadowed parts of this Chapter. It is a combination of two previous compositions. The first part was my first musical composition which evolved, over time, to become *Golden Ratio's Stability in Time and Space,* for I realized it was inspired by a pen and ink drawing by Leonardo Da Vinci titled Vitruvian Man—an image of a man enclosed in a circle and a square on the earth, symbolic of the Golden Ration.

The second part of that composition was formerly titled *Embrace the Mystery,* which was an expression of a poem dictated in a dream in April, 1990. Upon awakening, I grabbed a piece of paper and wrote it down:

Heavenly bodies of childhood
lose their brightness
with spoiled dreams, books,
and close-up photographs;
life becomes but a caricature,
like heavenly bodies.

You can take heart
if you want to marvel,
one phenomenon grows
with each encounter,
the human spirit,
greatest mystery of all.

Appreciate complexities
of survival, for no
spoiled dreams, books,
or close-up photographs
can take away the wonder
of that ascending power.

On March 13, 2018, I felt depressed and had no idea of what was wrong. Two days later Stephen Hawking's death was announced. Now I know that I was in sync with Hawking due to my admiration and compassion; he was only 18 months older than me.

It brought on another composition—Movement 4—*In Memory of Stephen Hawking, Albert Einstein, and Roger Wolcott Sperry.* Included in that movement is a former composition titled *Relative*

Time, inspired by Stephen Hawking many years ago. His death also brought on the writing of another poem (Appendix IV). A musical rendition of some verses of that poem was also included in that movement.

CHAPTER THREE

INTROSPECTION IS THE PATH TO INDIVIDUATION AND SELF-KNOWLEDGE

As said in Chapter One, Stephen Jay Gould's book, *The Mismeasure of Man,*[35] is a major contribution to the revolution of psychology. Throughout that book he reveals the subjectivity of the so-called scientists who were, and continue to be, the source of that mismeasurement, especially the selfish gene centered view of behavior promoted by author Richard Dawkins and Harvard Psychology Professor Steven Pinker.

Subjectivity is based on or influenced by personal feelings, tastes, or opinions, rather than facts. That selfish gene is the biological deterministic belief that human behavior is genetic.

There are, however, some scientists, like neuroendocrinology's Robert Sapolsky, bordering on the field of psychology, who, like Gould, protests that biological deterministic belief, evidenced in his writings, as well as his contribution to the 2011 documentary, *Zeitgeist, Moving Forward*. The belief that behavior is genetic is the fatalism to which Sperry was referring in the pathological field of psychology.

Gould also knew that we are inextricably part of nature and human uniqueness resides primarily in our brains. He found that the size of the human brain has not changed in over 50,000 years; human societies change by cultural evolution. He also stated that "'nothing but' an animal is as fallacious a statement as 'created in God's own image.'"

In his Introduction to *The Mismeasurement of Man,* Gould addresses the prejudices, including religion and that male god, which underlies the biological determinists' gene centered view of behavior. Those biological determinists invoked the traditional prestige of science as objective knowledge to support their prejudices, e.g., blacks are a separate race from whites, inheritance of intelligence … and the falsity of that so-called science. In his Acknowledgments Gould even addresses the sexist title of his book as a commentary on the biological determinists. "They did indeed study 'man' (that is, white European males), regarding this group as a standard and everybody else as something to be measured unfavorably against it. That they mismeasured 'man' underscores the double fallacy."

Gould also comments on Daniel J. Kelves' book, *In the Name of Eugenics,*[36] "The finest of all books on the history of eugenics." Kelves also addresses the social prejudices within that field as well as the destruction of humans in the name of eugenics, including the holocaust. In that book, JBS Haldane's 1924 opposition is evident in his complaint that genetic theory was being used in Britain "to support the political opinions of the extreme right and in America by some of the most ferocious enemies of human liberty."

Betty Edwards[37] was absolutely correct when she said the political right, which resists change, is associated with the sequential left brain, and the political left, which furthers change, is associated with the spatial right brain. As said before, conservatives who hold to traditional attitudes in politics, religion, as well as psychology, are responsible for the big divide between the left and right hemispheres of the brain.

Pertinent to the extreme right use of that genetic theory to maintain control over society in nineteenth century England is the awakening of Edwin A. Abbott's higher spatial brain capabilities. Abbott was a master teacher, theologian, and writer. His awakening is described in a memoir, disguised as a satirical novel, published in 1894, *Flatland, A Romance of Many Dimensions.*[38] It was published anonymously seven years after its initial writing. It would have been impossible for him to know the process of that major shift in consciousness, similar to mine, had he not actually experienced it. It is likely that the purpose of that publication was to acquire feedback to validate his experiences. After receiving critiques, he republished his memoir with a lengthy Preface regarding his errors as well as addressing insights regarding the numerous symbols in that initial writing.

For many years his book was generally ignored. It began to be republished in 1926, the year of his death. It has been republished many times since then. It has been the source of numerous commentaries and the inspiration for numerous books. One of the people he inspired was Claude Bragdon,[39] an architect, validating Bragdon's belief that space is a dimension of the mind. Bragdon also found that validation in the *I Ching*.

Those later publications of *Flatland* contain the subjectivity of its editors, words changed here and there, and Abbott's Preface to his second edition has often been omitted. The reason being that Preface exposes social and psychological issues—an underlying purpose of his writing—to bring positive change to humanity. Even in his initial writing Abbott ends his memoir with the hope that, in some future time, his words "may find their way to the minds of humanity."

Thomas F. Banchoff, professor of mathematics and the geometry of higher dimensions at Brown University, values Abbott's novella as a brilliantly conceived book. His statement regarding Abbott: "As a leader in the movement to provide educational opportunities for young men and women of all social classes, he was often frustrated by establishment views in education and religion. Of his fifty books, the one that still speaks clearly to our own day is his little masterpiece, *Flatland,* simultaneously a social satire and an introduction to the idea of higher dimensions." [40]

Basic to the dimensions in Abbott's novel, Flatland is dominated by the sequential left brain, and Spaceland is reflective of higher spatial right brain capabilities.

In his revealing Preface, Abbott speaks of dimensions beyond Spaceland. He argues that dimension implies direction and measurement and when we go beyond direction and measurement, we cannot know what to measure or in what direction. Yet he believes it to be there. He is speaking of the life force, which manifests in the human spirit, when he says, "Even I cannot comprehend it, nor realize it by the sense of sight or by any process of reason; I can but apprehend it by faith."

Abbott also elucidates his thoughts on patriarchal hierarchy, "those who maintain superiority over multitude of their countrymen by their intellectual power are in conflict with nature; nature in sentencing them to infecundity [lack of creativity] has condemned them to ultimate failure." He also states, "I see a fulfillment of the great law of all worlds, that while the wisdom of man thinks it is working one thing, the wisdom of nature constrains it to work another and quite a different and far better thing."

He dedicates his book to the inhabitants of space in general [those insightful and spiritual people] "so the citizens of that celestial region may aspire yet higher and higher to the secrets of four, five, or even six dimensions thereby contributing to the imagination and the possible development of that most rare and excellent gift of modesty among the superior races of solid humanity."

Abbott's Preface continues in order to acknowledge two major errors in his book, in response to those critiques—one of an intellectual nature, the other one moral—and addresses the corrections. The intellectual two-dimensional concept of flatland is actually three. He reports that during the years of contemplating his experiences, the immoral sexist implications toward women and irregulars changed.

Taken as a whole, his use of the words, on the one hand and on the other hand, indicates that he is dealing with conflict between his two hemispheres. The seven years of imprisonment [enmeshment/ entrapment] in Flatland, was spent attempting to overcome the impediments to unity and equality.

Abbott's claim to have written Flatland as a historian is congruent with his two dimensional concept of Flatland, for history is available in the educational system in the two dimensional world of books. Those books, in leaving out the dark side of human history, essentially become lies. While he uses geometry to represent the numerous social dimensions of the sequential measurement of human worth, he demonstrates extreme focus on details, which makes it difficult to see the big picture. It is an example of an old saying—one cannot see the forest for the trees.

Abbott divides his novel into two parts, *This World* and *Other Worlds.*

In Part One, Abbott's protagonist, a Square, initiates the reader into This World and the inhabitants—geometric figures—and the strictly divided castes of Flatland society. Those social groups are determined by the number and size of the inhabitants' angles.

Circles are the most esteemed of castes, the high priests of the various subjects in Flatland. The circles dictate conformity: irregulars, those with uneven sides and shapes are of the lowest class of males. They are gotten rid of or imprisoned or assigned to some menial, meaningless task. Anyone in Flatland who entertains the notion of dimensions higher than This World is also eliminated or imprisoned.

Women are straight lines; they are the lowest and most pitiable caste, having no angles or any hope of bettering their positions. Their miseries and humiliation are believed to be a result of natural laws or the product of evolution—that biological determinist view.

In Flatland, evolution to a higher status is usually accomplished by males with even sides. The irregulars, like women, are considered predestined to hopelessness.

The ambient condition in Flatland is primary darkness, exacerbated by the fog, which the Square describes as comforting and necessary to the maintenance of the caste structure of society. The fog [of prejudice] diminishes sensate existence.

After familiarizing the reader to life in This World, the Square, in Part Two, narrates his Introduction to Other Worlds, dimensions that lie both beneath and above the limited environment of Flatland. In his movement toward enlightenment, the Square encounters the revealing world of dreams, ideas, along with the vicissitudes that accompany contradictions to his familiar existence.

In his first dream of dimensions other than This World, the Square is introduced to Lineland where the populace consists of lines and points moving in a single direction, and each can only see the point immediately in front of or behind it. Women are the points, and the lines are males with two different voices on either end, used to attract two wives, each of whom has a voice that harmonizes with one end of the line or the other.

Lineland is obviously an underlying dimension of Flatland. As said in the previous Chapter, that creation of women as the second sex is in the biblical book of Genesis. Women were supposedly created by that jealous god to pleasure men and to procreate.

The next event of his awakening was a vision of a circle which transforms into a sphere, the character assigned to his spatial brain. The circle, though, arouses fear and the forbidden emotion of anger toward the high priests of each subject dominating This World. Abbott then begins to hear a voice in his mind, like the Sphere addressing the eye inside—insight. His spatial brain had taken charge. The Square describes his initial experience of space:

"An unspeakable horror seized me. There was a darkness; then a dizzy, sickening sensation of sight that was not like seeing; I saw a Line that was no Line; Space that was not Space: I was myself, and not myself. When I could find voice, I shrieked aloud in agony: Either this is madness or it is Hell."

His inner Spaceland voice comes again, "It is neither, it is knowledge." As he slowly adapts to that vision of the character of his spatial brain, the Square is seized by a religious experience and perceives the Sphere as god. It takes some time before he realizes the Sphere is not a god; then the insight that he can only adjust to change by degrees. Another insight—as the illusions of his life began to topple—the shallowness of Flatland and his former blindness.

The square feels empowered by that new-found capacity to see; then the Sphere's voice, "Does this omnividence make you more just, more merciful, less selfish, more loving?" To which the Square replies in shock, "More merciful, more loving, but these are the qualities of women." His spatial brain's question arouses the insight that the wisest women think more of humane values and authentic feelings than of understanding, more of the despised Straight Lines than of the esteemed Circles.

Subsequent to the Square's acceptance of the higher dimension that had been rendered unconscious, he becomes exhilarated with thought progression, an arrogance that sends him back to Flatland. That return evokes another dream in which he encounters the lowest depth of existence—the nonmoving, non-dimensional, "vile and ignorant" land of the Point. The single inhabitant of the land of the

Point is completely self-contained, self-satisfied, and oblivious of any dimension other than his own; he attributes all existence to his own thought, unable to see, to hear, to move, or to change. In his dream, the Square is astounded at such complacency and, try as he might, he is unable to budge him. His spatial brain stops the futile efforts with the words: "There is nothing that you or I can do to rescue him from his self-satisfaction."

That dream is a major point of Abbott's book. It validated my insight that complacency maintains the shallow, oppressive, and spiritless human world dominated by the sequential left brain.

Within Abbott's writing are his discoveries of spatial brain attributes much higher than imagination: valid emotions, creativity, humane values, and the capacity to see the big picture—a holistic view. Another validation was his discovery that it is the eye inside [insight] which evolves consciousness. That, together with the human spirit, over time, can take one to the highest level—the celestial region of the mind.

Abbott's Flatland also validates the contents of *The Sacred Canopy,*[41] written by Sociologist Peter L. Berger. In his book Berger asserts that religion serves to legitimize social, economic, political, and cultural traditions of a society.

Religion evolved into Social Constructionism, a term associated with Berger. It is "a school of thought pertaining to the way social phenomena are created, institutionalized, and made into tradition by humans."[42] Berger also knew that religion has wormed its way into every nook and cranny of human society, especially that school of thought. Abbott's description of women's shortcomings in Flatland is also a validation of Berger's assertion that religion has resulted in a religious woman's tendency toward non-sexual masochism—tolerance of abuse and oppression. Women were not even allowed to vote in the U.S. until 1920.

Both Abbott and Berger confirm Stephen Jay Gould's work regarding the double fallacy of biological determinism. Abbott confirms more of Gould's insights: humans are inextricably part of nature; human uniqueness resides primarily in our brains; the dominance of the fog of prejudice resulting in the mismeasure of humans is still evident in the current flatland field of psychology as well as society at large. There are no female theorists acknowledged other than those who are enmeshed in the pathological field of psychology.

Abbott's book does, unfortunately, speak clearly to our own day regarding that gene centered view of behavior, which continues to contribute to our predominantly patriarchal and materialistic sequential left-brain world. It is also evidenced by the contributors to Daniel C. Maguire and Sa' Diyya Shaikh's revealing book, *Violence Against Women in Contemporary World Religions*[43] in the 21st century. It is an example of hell on earth created by religion, even Buddhism.

Another confirmation is from those ancient sages in the *I Ching*. Hexagram #23 is *Splitting Apart*, which means ruin. Inferior left brain people have gone too far in adornment and overcoming the spatial hemisphere's functioning. Hexagram #24, *Return* is of the spatial brain, which leads to self-knowledge.

* * *

Another significant man was found who works to make positive changes to the human world—anthropologist and physician Dr. Paul Farmer. Essentially, he confronts the inequities of human constructionism in his book, *Pathologies of Power: Health, Human Rights, and the New War on the Poor.*[44] It is an eye-opening book and provides numerous examples of the pathologies of the use of power in high places resulting in structural violence—the way by which social arrangements are constructed to put specific members of a population in harm's way.

Dr. Farmer is the founder of *Partners in Health,* which began with his humanitarian work in Haiti and now extends throughout the world. He is a man who has truly made a difference in the lives of countless people, especially those who could perish from lack of basic human needs, even food and water.

Paul Farmer is dedicated to the philosophy that "the only real nation is humanity."[45]

Although Farmer is still somewhat connected with Catholicism, he is aware of the inequities, that evil oppression, existing within that patriarchal system. His awareness is evident in his support of Liberation Theology, a movement initiated during the 1950s in South America by Catholic priests whose focus was on the suffering of the poor and disenfranchised, even women, and an attempt to evolve Christianity to include humanitarian ideals.

It was a movement, though, that was thwarted by the Vatican that condemned it as being Marxist; the same Vatican that provided escape routes for Nazi war criminals who committed monstrous crimes against humanity.

* * *

My first book, *Of Golden Frogs and Such, A Story of Survival and Transformation,* 2006, was, like Abbott's book, a memoir regarding my awakening; it was written as a case study, in hope of obtaining feedback, for there was nothing in the field of psychology to explain what was happening to my mind other than Carl Jung's "the coming of the unconscious."[46] Each chapter began with one of my 1990 poems, for I had discovered that they were directives to achieve mental health.

At the time of that writing I had no access to the internet, and could not find knowledge of Roger Wolcott Sperry's ongoing accomplishments anywhere, even libraries. I had, however, discovered Pierre Janet's work. He coined the words, *dissociation* and *subconscious,* and the first theorist, over a century ago, to know there is a connection between events in the subject's past and his or her present-day symptoms.

Subconscious is: of or concerning the part of the mind of which one is not fully aware but which influences one's actions or feeling. It is essentially events in one's past available for recall when attention is drawn to them. Abbott's, *A Romance of Many Dimensions,* did draw attention to the Flatland field of psychology as well as the Flatland in which I had lived most of my life, especially in my family of origin. Examining my life was directed by another April, 1990 poem:

Spirit requires a disciplined mind
with faithfulness of purpose
for revelation to be complete.

To deviate, mind does forsake
and calculates to seek,
with ease, another story.

It looks in another's face
to find flaws it would hide,
its own mirror points the finger.

Past is dead I would believe,
now it's time, truth to seek,
mistakenly without discomfort.

Mirror, in that poem, was a major symbol in many dreams, as well as poems. I finally came to realize that it was symbolic of self-reflection.

Raised by a fundamental Christian mother and a secular controlling father, I essentially lived as a slave on the family farm in rural Sumter County, Florida, as did my younger brother and older sister. My brother was the only one in the family with whom I formed a bond of love. His birth, when I was 6 years old, aroused an early awakening of the instinct to protect one's child. I attempted, unsuccessfully, to protect him from the physical and mental abuse imposed by our parents. He was one of the sweetest children I had ever known. His resulting mental dysfunction was alcoholism.

My first marriage, at age 19, provided an escape from that dysfunctional family. Over time that husband became oppressive in many ways, especially preventing me from taking college courses as well as criticizing my music; he was even jealous of our daughter, born when I was 21. I left him in 1970 with my beloved daughter. Three years later we moved to Winter Park, Florida; a move which was a major change, for I had the opportunity to begin college.

My brother's mental dysfunction strongly influenced my decision to major in psychology and become a counsellor. I was also determined to leave a different legacy for my daughter.

The writing of that first book was necessary to resolve another bitter period of my life: a misogynist psychologist who attempted to destroy my life. At the root of misogyny is jealousy. That psychologist was a member of the Quaker Church and an anti-war advocate. He was recommended by a colleague as a therapist for my intelligent husband—the romantic love of my life—who was born in communist Poland. He had been told by his architectural boss that he had to work on communication and empathy. During a session attended with my husband at the request of that psychologist, he suggested that I make an individual appointment with him.

When my strange and disturbing dreams began in January, 1990, I did make an appointment, for I wanted to discuss them with a professional. The next 18 months associated with that evil man was a nightmare experience; fortunately, everything was recorded in my journal. He had encouraged hope for a better understanding. He had condemned my marriage by saying that my husband was attempting to drive me crazy. At the time, I thought that he knew something that I did not, which resulted in a divorce. Essentially that was a projection, for that therapist was making that attempt. He said that I was not as strong as I thought I was and could never work again if I did not do as he said. He was a believer in the false recovered memory fad, and through so-called metaphors made me wonder if I had been sexually abused by my father.

In re-reading my journal in 1993, I found another poem which revealed that I knew, unconsciously, that he was, indeed, an evil, spiritless man:

Disembodied memories
paint surrealistic pictures
to disturb my soul,
yearning to escape
unspoken, broken pieces.

Specter from hell,
taunt me no more
with bewitching intentions
of unspoken, broken
pieces.

Attend your own
pale countenance
seeking to dissect
me to find your
elusive soul.

In reviewing my journal I realized why I kept returning to sessions for counselling. That psychologist's actions and words recorded in my journal revealed the concept of enmeshment:

Enmeshment is the persuasive brain-washing by which the person in the position of authority—whether it be a parent, companion, teacher, theorist, therapist, president, priest, preacher, guru, pandit, gang leader, Ron Hubbard, Adolf Hitler, or Osama bin Laden, in order to gain power and control over other people. Patriarchal religions, founded in animalistic sex and aggression, have always been about power and control. In Christianity, control is accomplished by the threat of hell and the carrot of heavenly reward.

Need is a prerequisite for vulnerability to enmeshment. That need may be a basic physiological necessity or safety needs; it may be an esteem need, social need, need for a sense of purpose. It is a given that all children are vulnerable.

Another part of the enmeshment process is punishment and reward—the promise of need fulfillment to maintain focus. Punishment plays on the fears of people; intimidation, both subtle and obvious, is also a part of that scheme.

The most effective strategy, though, is isolation. That isolation is accomplished by condemning or scapegoating people who threaten the agenda or beliefs of those in position of power, thereby thwarting any dissenting voice. It is a well-known fact that condemnation—the root of hatred and prejudice—is taught. One becomes mentally, and sometimes physically isolated from those who have a different point of view. Isolation is a significant symptom that coercion is taking place.

It was an esteem need that made me vulnerable. That evil psychologist discounted all the people who could have intervened in his destruction. When he attempted to separate me from my daughter, my spatial brain took charge and dictated actions that released me from that enmeshment. It was a week later that my awakening vision occurred. During that dark period of my life, my fortitude is obvious, for I did not fail to achieve daily tasks, especially positive care for my clients.

After the horrendous experience with that evil psychologist, the death of my father and a client, as well as my brother's suffering from a tragic incident, I needed to take a break from my counselling work. When my ex-husband was fired from his job, he called to tell me that he had a new job that required his return to Poland.

I moved to Poland to be with my former husband and achieved a part-time job in the Psychology Department of a local university in Bialystok Poland in September 1992. The director considered my work successful. He said it resulted in evolving consciousness. It was the first time I ever heard that phrase.

As time moved on, I realized that my husband had changed. Essentially he became re-enmeshed in fundamental Catholicism evidenced in hatred of Jews and lack of humane values. Due to that enmeshment he had a mind raped by the threat of hell, as well as a sexual raping in his youth by a Catholic priest.

A two page writing in April 1992 was included in *Of Golden Frogs and Such.* It, like my music, was a self-fulfilling prophecy. Eventually

I became aware it was the intertwining of numerous concerns in my unconscious mind, including the pathology of psychology, religious prejudices, the destruction of our life-sustaining planet, the waste of human life in the holocaust, as well as grief. That brief writing, titled *My Golden Frog*, ended with a sense of purpose: writing and nourishing consciousness of the human spirit. I left Poland two months later, June 14, 1992. Grief was ahead of me, for when I left my beloved companion at the airport, I felt as though my heart was breaking.

That first book also recorded my experience working as a group counsellor at The Center for Drug Free Living, in Orlando, Florida during 1996-7. My work was in opposition to the biological determinist therapists who also worked there. I began each session with body stretches and relaxation. I advanced self-knowledge in the group by requiring a brief writing of their personal history, as well as journaling and drawings. I taught them about the life force, the human spirit, which made us all sisters and brothers of the phenomenal human species. Essentially, I felt great compassion for each of them.

One of those clients gave me a precious gift on August 6, 1997, *Life's Little Treasure Book ON WISDOM,*[47] inscribed with a personal note, "Dear Frances: I hope that life gives back to you what you so generously give away. Thank you for everything."

My brother supposedly hanged himself in the Sumter County jail on September 11, 1998, found in an article in the Sumter County Times. I knew, though, that he was a victim of multidimensional evil, including the Pentecostal (Church of God) religious sheriff of Sumter County, as well as some of his so-called counsellors, who believed that his alcoholism was genetic. That sheriff lied about Charlie's death when he told my mother that he had a heart attack in the jail cell. My brother's rage and frustration was evident when drunk. While some people considered him dangerous, others experienced his sober kindness and believed that he was not suicidal.

The writing of that first book was, indeed, a story of transformation, as well as individuation, for I was no longer enmeshed in religion or the pathological field of psychology. It gave value to my brother's life; our bond of love had continued, for he, like me, was fascinated with nature and music. He could sing beautifully and taught himself to play a harmonica.

The first strange and disturbing dream, foreshadowing my poetry and awakening, occurred on my brother's birthday, January 27, 1990. The symbols and meaning of the dream was that I had been fed a lot of shit in my life, but some I would not swallow by either brain was the Christian perception that everyone is born evil. My spatial brain was essentially telling me that my beloved brother was born innocent. At his funeral, I read a published article that he had written seven years before his death. (Appendix III). Also provided Bob Dylan's music, *The Answer My Friend, Is Blowin in the Wind,* for others to hear his favorite song at the end of the funeral.

That first book was also an attempt to warn others of the danger of psycho-therapy.

* * *

After my brother's death, I composed *A Winter's Night,* which helped me to overcome grief. It was also symbolic of rising above the bitter side of his life. That song, like most of my music, seemed as though my left and right hemispheres were communicating with each other through my two hands—especially my love and compassion for Charlie and the value of his life to me. When I orchestrated that original piano composition to be the first part of Movement 2, I was amazed at its beauty and titled it *With Love and Compassion We can Rise Above the Bitter Side of Life.*

The second part of that Concerto was titled *A Mother's Song,* which symbolized love for my daughter. It was also inspired by another poem written in September, 1990:

> Darkened, that face of mine
> with the sleep of death,
> forty years, frozen
> tears did mummify.
>
> Words spoken through the mask,
> tight lips did murmur,
> please release my soul
> to fulfill my task.
>
> An endless line a circle made,
> colored with rich bright rose;
> across its girth a blackened blade
> with a double edge.
>
> It spoke to me of endless love
> so rich, pure, and innocent,
> it would carve in timeless space

the true strong sign of mother.

Oh sisters, if I could only
tell the beauty of that love
and our painful, giving task,
the true strong sign of mother.

Sever the golden chord you hold,
release your sons and daughters;
they are not for your comfort made
nor for your guilt to carry.

Give them instead the gift of rose
and with the blade across your breast,
endure your own magnificence;
live as their example.

Those frozen tears was a suppression of the grief imposed by my parents. Rose is often a cultural symbol of love. The vision revealed that true love for my daughter was at the root of my motivation for change.

The mask, in that poem, was a mystery, yet an image of it suddenly appeared in my mind months later, an image I was compelled to draw. Even that drawing was a mystery, evidently evoked by my spatial brain. Its symbolic meaning became evident during those years of introspection and initial writing of my memoir. It was an image of enmeshment in religion—the raping of the mind.

Severing the golden chord was a directive to free my daughter from enmeshment and to support freedom of choice regarding her own life. Her life has become successful in multiple dimensions, especially supporting fulfillment of human needs and humane values. She is also creative and a very loving mother.

* * *

The intertwining of everything has been evidenced in the 6th[th] Movement of my Concerto, titled *Reflections on Peak Experiences.* It contains revised versions of parts of two separate songs, *A Winter's Night* and *Reflections on Majdanek.* I found similarities in those compositions. The revision is a change from minor to major keys.

A major peak experience occurred at Majdanek, the memorial of a Nazi death camp bordering on the city of Lublin Poland. My feelings evoked the insight that we are all sisters and brothers of the phenomenal human species. It also evidenced that those destroyed humans, like my brother, never had the chance to live full lives.

That peak experience also evoked a vow to never be silent again. The fulfillment of that vow has fully changed my life. My love and compassion has helped me to rise above the truly bitter side of life produced by horrific left brain humans.

SELF-ACTUALIZATION: EVER RISING IS TRUE BEING

Humanist psychologist Abraham Harold Maslow was a victim of the fog of prejudice in his early years, for his parents were first generation Jewish immigrants from Russia. He experienced Anti-Semitism from his teachers and from other children in his neighborhood in Brooklyn, New York. Anti-Semitic gang members even attacked him physically. His home was also a source of oppression due to disagreements with his selfish and prejudiced mother. Without friends, he essentially grew up in libraries and among books, developing a love for books and learning. It becomes obvious that his early life experiences played a major role in his hierarchy of human needs: physiological, safety, social, esteem, and self-actualization.

It is also obvious that another need should be added—intellectual. That capacity to learn, think, and to question everything in order to achieve individuation, helped him to overcome the deficiency of safety needs as well as the social need for love and affection.

Maslow's hierarchy of human needs and human values were only the beginning of his mental achievements. Through his own peak experiences, he moved on, through evolution of consciousness, to Holism. His peak experiences are synonymous with insight. While all functioning humans use both brains, it is insight, "the capacity to discern the true nature of a situation; penetration,"[48] which evolves consciousness.

While Maslow lacked knowledge of spatial and sequential brain functioning, it is obvious that his B [humane] values emanate from the spatial right brain, and D [deficiency] values regarding human needs, are sequential left brain challenges. His next move was to transpersonal psychology and self-transcendence, that celestial region of the mind, to borrow Abbott's term.

Maslow's enlightenment and self-actualization is a major contribution to the revolution of psychology. He was like those revolutionary Chaos scientists, especially his top-down view as well as his innate right brain capacity to see patterns across different scales at the same time. Maslow made quantum leaps in his theories. Like those scientists, his accomplishments were derided. He was accused of lacking science in his conclusions. He was also disparaged by the sequential right wing conservatives, especially Christina Hoff Sommers, social critic, and Sally Satel, a truly psychopathic practicing psychiatrist, who says that Maslow's ideas are no longer taken seriously in the world of academic psychology. Unfortunately, that is true; in my education he was only mentioned in connection with Humanist psychologist Carl Rogers, among the founding members of client centered psychotherapy. Sommers and Satel were the authors of *One Nation Under Therapy: How the Helping Culture is Eroding Self-reliance,*[49] the consequence of their attacks on the human-potential movement—a mid-20th-century offspring of psychologists Abraham Maslow and Carl Rogers and the parent, in turn, of the self-esteem craze.

There are, however, some educational programs, outside of Universities, that teach Humanistic and Holistic Psychology, like Doris Jeanette, PsyD, who teaches "The New Holistic Psychology" in Philadelphia (available online). As she knows, even some of those trained in Holistic psychology subjectively maintain traditional suppressive psycho-therapy.

Maslow's top-down view of mental health is in contrast to the focus on mental illness. He based his work on people who evidenced self-actualization: Albert Einstein, Dr. Albert Schweitzer, anthropologist Ruth Benedict, Gestalt psychologist Max Wertheimer, Henry David Thoreau, poet, philosopher, naturalist, and abolitionist, as well as Lao Tzu, an ancient Chinese philosopher and writer who was greatly influenced by the *I Ching*.

All of his examples of self-actualized people were aware of reality, in contrast to those who distort the world to fit with their beliefs. They were, as well, aware of the human connection with nature. They, like Maslow, evidenced differentiation and individuation, terms used by Systems Theorist and Psychiatrist Murray Bowen, also ignored in my education. Bowen used degrees of differentiation *as* a measure of mental health in order to achieve individuation from one's family.

Broadly, *individuation* is the process of becoming a separate individual, using one's capacity to think, feel, speak, and act on one's own—the movement away from mental dependence. While Bowen's concept has validity, he does not address the source of that mental dependence—enmeshment.

* * *

The first poem conceived in April, 1990 was:
Word aphasia,
even brained,
an oddity.

Countless thoughts
locked inside,
no words could tell.

They tumble out,
and the taste
is bitter-sweet.

I had learned in graduate school that, generally, those with above average intelligence rank higher, by at least 20 points, on either spatial or sequential tasks as determined by the Wechsler IQ Test. The attainment of equal scores is rare, which happened to apply to me. Yet committing words, and even my music, to memory was, and still is, incredibly difficult for me. Words and sounds are overridden by images in my mind, what Linda Kreger Silverman terms a *visual-spatial learner* in her 2002 book, *Upside down Brilliance: The Visual Spatial Learner.*[50] In her book she contrasts Visual-Spatial [right brain] abilities with Auditory-Sequential [left-brain] skills, a listing she offers to the public via the internet. (Appendix II) The even-brained oddity, though, presented a challenge throughout my life— interested in and curious about EVERYTHING. It even provoked travel to many foreign countries. Many times, I have been regarded as a Renaissance woman, capable of doing everything.

That even brained oddity is obviously applicable to people of wisdom, including the ancient sages. While Silverman's listing is applicable to learning, the higher spatial brain abilities picks up where she ended the visual spatial learning: "Is creatively, technologically, mechanically, emotionally or spiritually gifted; Is a late bloomer." Late blooming is due to ongoing evolution of consciousness.

The following is the result of research and experience:

Sequential Left Brain	Spatial Right Brain
Verbal orientation and language	Visual orientation and symbolism
Human Needs: physical, safety, social, esteem, and intellectual	Spirituality: fortitude and reverence for life
Subconscious	
Attention to Details	Holistic View
Logical/rational	Intuition—the capacity to discern patterns
Reality	Imagination, Creativity, Technology
Hedonistic values: pleasures of the five senses	Humane values: honesty/sincerity, compassion/kindness, justice/fairness, wisdom
External physical awareness	Internal physical awareness

Capacity to focus

After the imposition of
patriarchy and religion,
the sequential left
brain accepted beliefs
as facts resulting in:

Belief Orientation

Ego: beliefs about
ones' self, resulting in
inflated feelings of pride
and superiority

Learned prejudices;
Subjectivity

Learned feelings   Authentic emotions

Mythological beliefs, imposed by religion and human constructionism—prejudices—as well as massive egos, override higher spatial brain abilities, rendering them unconscious. Even awareness of human needs are suppressed by egotistic people.

In contrast, consciousness, the sequential and spatial hemispheres, united by the human spirit, results in self-actualization, wholeness, and modesty, which overrides the ego. Insight, as well, requires both hemispheres and can be obtained by introspection, "Contemplation of one's own thoughts, feelings, and sensations; self-examination."[51] Dreams, though, are the major source of insight, as evidenced in Edwin A. Abbott's and my awakening. Even now, I awaken each morning with increased clarification.

As noted in the last words of *A Psalm of Wisdom,* Appendix I, for insight we must learn to wait.

True being is evidenced in my description of mental health. While no one is perfect, it is the quality of functioning for which one should strive:

> Mental health is balanced wholeness: one's sequential and spatial brains, body, and behavior unified by the human spirit, living separately but together with other people.
>
> The healthy reflect stability, which is rooted in reality and the detailed, sequential side of living as well as the capacity to focus. It is being responsible for one's daily life. With that firm foundation one evidences flexibility to cope with change, both bitter and sweet, which is a part of living.
>
> The healthy reflect insight attained through introspection and engaging the creative spatial brain's capacity to see the big picture—holistic perception—and the ability to discern patterns; engaging, as well, the spatial brain's authentic emotions, inner body awareness, and firm humane principles beginning with the essentials of honesty and sincerity.
>
> Within the process of using all of those natural powers and abilities, one discovers and engages

unique talents and the fulfillment of one's potential; discovering as well, one's sense of purpose.

Like Maslow, I learned that the purpose of therapy is to help clients to overcome impediments to wholeness. That realization began during my internship at a mental health center in Sumter County. A client, labeled with schizophrenia, did not evidence psychosis in our session. I discussed it with the supervisor; he said the client responded to the way I conceived him. It was a conception influenced by my brother's history.

After receiving my license as a mental health counsellor, I opened a private practice in Maitland, Florida, which became increasingly successful through referrals from clients, colleagues, and a psychiatrist who appreciated my insightful work with his patients. That success had nothing to do with money, for therapy fees were altered for clients lacking insurance or financial stability. That success, though, increased over the years, for it was not only achieved through insight, but through intuition and compassion for my clients. Many of my clients spoke of the positive changes in their lives; e.g., one who wrote me a note saying, "Thank you for helping me find my life." I was surprised when another one gave me a photograph of an angel statue in a cemetery and wrote on the back of it, "To Francis, my angel."

As said before, I did not perceive my clients as mentally ill, but victims of violence, physical, emotional, and structural—essentially wounded and oppressed. The only time I labeled a client was to fulfill the insurance requirement of diagnosis; adjustment disorder was the only one used.

Another April 1990 poem regarded my own feelings and unconscious knowledge:

Despair I attempted to evade,
the word that suicide is made of,
the facing of the truth of evil,
no chance of reconciliation.

Children bear the horror,
the damage goes unseen;
silent, killing evil does exist
in the eyes of complacency.

Turn the other cheek from the vomit,
the child cannot stomach the horror;
call it mental illness, label it instead,
destruction of this society.

The client who inspired that poem was artistic, yet she exhibited the symptom of bulimia. Her plight touched me deeply. She often brought clippings and drawings to our sessions, and the theme of those visual images seemed to be of abandoned, neglected, and battered children. Over months of exploring and talking about those pictures, she gradually began to acknowledge the violence and terror that filled her early years. While the symptom of eating then vomiting was rarely addressed, she began to discover its symbolic meaning. She had been forced to "swallow" her feelings, and she was compelled to expel what was inside of her. Ever so gradually she began to own her feelings and to feel her mental pain—the grief that was inevitable. Finally, an exceptional day came; she rushed into the room, almost late for her appointment, carrying a sack of fast food and a soft drink. Curling up in her chair she said, "Didn't have time to eat," and proceeded to consume a large hamburger, fries, and a jumbo drink, talking between bites and sips. As she began to leave at the end of the session, she asked, "Did it bother you that I ate in your office?" I replied with an emphatic "Yes," then "Please do not bring food into this office without bringing some for me." We laughed together, and I gave her a hug. Then she told me that bulimic and other fearful symptoms were gone. I already knew that individuals with bulimia prefer not to eat in front of other people.

I finally found, within neurological science, validation of my knowledge that clients were often victims of violence, physical, emotional, and structural. Even schizophrenia is associated with abuse. In a 2009 overview of competing theories of Schizophrenia by K. M. Vekquin,[52] is the "Traumagenic Neurodevelopmental Model." It associates the onset of the symptoms with tremendous and chronic inhumane violence. It is a model that has been acknowledged as "the most scientifically rigorous and logically consistent" in other countries, but not the U.S. What those researchers failed to see, though, is that emotional violence can be just as devastating.

Vekquin does, however, confirm that grief is a major pathway to redeeming one's life when he says that healing the wounds invoked by violence requires a therapist with the "therapeutic skill to not only withstand, but to be a gentle guide through the profound sorrow, grief, rage, and terror that results in transcendence of the psychosis."

I also became conscious of the value of writing therapy notes, for, over time, patterns of behaviors, thoughts, and feelings would emerge. That insight inspired my journaling. My intuitive work progressed; when someone had difficulty expressing themselves or what they were feeling, I began to hand them a piece of paper and asked them to draw. It seemed obvious to me that the HTP psychological test, comprised of drawing a house, a tree, and a person, often revealed symbols of subconscious experiences as well as unconscious spatial brain knowledge. Even the simplest drawing, like a dream, can "reveal much about you to yourself, some facets of you that are obscured by your verbal self," to quote Betty Edwards. Her book, *Drawing on the Right Side of the Brain,*[53] validated so much of what I knew intuitively.

As said before regarding Edwin A. Abbott's and my awakening, a basic source of insight is dreams. Dreams are evoked by the parietal lobe, behind the frontal lobes. The parietal lobe is involved in the integration of spatial and sequential sensory information, essentially bringing synthesis to the information received by both the left and right hemispheres. Most dreaming occurs during the fourth stage of sleep, known as rapid eye movement (REM) sleep. REM sleep is characterized by eye movement, increased respiration rate, and increased brain activity.

One of the reasons that dreams are ignored by some psycho-therapists is the difficulty of interpreting symbols contained in the dreams. Only the dreamer can know the meaning of the symbols. Symbols are produced by the creative spatial brain, yet are indicative of something happening in the present or something that has happened in the past that has not been resolved; it continues in the subconscious mind to affect behavior. Dreams frequently contain authentic emotions as well as intuition.

An example of an intuitive dream was evidenced by a child. She described a frightening dream of her father becoming a changeling. In reply to my question regarding her fear, she said that she was in no danger but was worried. A week after that dream, her father was placed in a psychiatric hospital. She knew something was different in her father's general patterns of behavior even though she did not comprehend what was happening.

Some of my poetry evoked by my spatial brain in a dream took time to understand the symbolic meaning.

* * *

Another poem I have written was placed at the ending of my third book, *Flatland, Spaceland, and Beyond: The Wisdom of Nature,* 2013. The writing of that book brought on a utopian life for me, which resulted in my fourth book, *Empowered Humans: The Phenomenon of Being.* I had overcome the manmade impediments to wholeness.

The words of that poem were evoked by a piano composition. Like many of my compositions, I was outside in my flower garden when music was heard in my mind. That particular time, what I heard was changing chords, symbolic of change that comes from inside. I rushed inside to record those chords and more music came through both of my hands, evoking my sequential brain's verbal orientation. The music's title is *Ode to Being:*

Through space and time

I stand undaunted
in the guiding light
of all nature.

Gone, the chains
of human myth;
free to be
all that I am.

The joy that
freedom brings
grows richer
each day.

Extolling harmony
and the gift of life;
ever rising
is true Being.

That music has now been fully orchestrated, the third movement
of my Concerto.

CHAPTER FIVE:

THE EMERGENT MIND AND THE ASCENDING POWER WITHIN

As Roger Wolcott Sperry knew, we need humane values to bring positive change to our human world. Humanitarianism and spirituality are also inextricably intertwined. The cosmic life force, which manifests in the human spirit, is the ascending power within.

As said in Chapter Two, Sperry's concept of the emergent mind is evolution of consciousness. He also addresses the mind-body connection:

> Consciousness emerges from the activity of cerebral networks as an independent entity. This newly emerged property which we call "mind" or "consciousness," continually feeds back to the central nervous system, resulting in a highly dynamic process of emergence, feedback (downward causation), newly emergent states, further feedback, and so forth. Reducing consciousness to its separate components obliterates the emergent phenomenon of "mind" with all its great power and uniqueness.

The central nervous system consists of the brain and spinal cord. The brain plays a central role in the control of most bodily functions, including awareness, movements, sensations, thoughts, speech, and memory.[54]

That creeping materialism Sperry addresses regarding the pathological field of psychology, not only affects the human mind, it even affects the food we eat and the air we breathe. As neuroendocrinology's Robert Sapolsky revealed in his 2008 documentary, *Stress, Portrait of a Killer,* stress can occur in one's job, especially in the lower caste of the business. Violence also plays a major role in stress. It was evident in many of my clients who had been oppressed and/or abused. Stress definitely affects the mind and consciousness, as well as the body.

Sapolsky's documentary is even more memorable when he exhibits his research revealing that stress even affects the fetus in the womb.

As said in Chapter One, the contributions of many other men have contributed to my emergent mind. Sapolsky's documentary allowed me to become conscious of why I had suffered from numerous serious illnesses as a teenager in my abusive home environment.

Henry Wadsworth Longfellow's *A Psalm of Life,* discovered when I was sixteen, had a major effect on my mind. I memorized the first three and the last verse of that initial poem and often said it to myself when frustrated.

Tell me not in mournful numbers
Life is but an empty dream,
For the soul is dead that slumbers

And things are not what they seem.

Life is real, Life is earnest,
And the grave is not its goal.
Dust thou are, to dust returneth,
Was not spoken of the soul.

Not enjoyment and not sorrow
Is our destined end or way,
But to act that each tomorrow
Find us further than today.

Let us then, be up and doing,
With a heart for any fate,
Still achieving, still pursuing,
Learn to labor and to wait.

The first two verses brought on an event in my teenage years: Sitting in the darkness on a grassy knoll, gazing at the night sky, my wish was made on all the stars of the cosmos: "Please, oh please, let me be all that I can be." The third verse brought on writing numerous pages regarding a higher plane of existence and tapping into a higher consciousness. Those pages were destroyed when my mother threatened to send me to a state mental institution. That higher plane of existence had also evoked a dream of remodeling an old southern mansion. The upper story had a comfortable safe room as well as a beautiful spacious room with a grand piano and large art easel. Time for practicing piano and art had not been allowed.

The last verse gave support to my connection with nature obtained by working so much on the family farm. I essentially became a workaholic by also doing yard work, cooking, learning to sew, and learning to play clarinet at school. There has not been a time in my ongoing life that I have not had a project.

When my awakening occurred in 1991, my first thought was that the event was what I had been waiting for most of my life.

Just before leaving Bialystok, Poland, in 1993, I conceived a 14-page writing regarding the reflective human. It was evoked by books I took with me when I made that major move. The books must have been chosen by my unconscious mind, for they contained knowledge needed to give credence to my fascination with nature, as well as the pathology of psychology: James Gleick's *Chaos,*[55] Leonard Shlain's *Art & Physics,*[56] Psychiatrist Henri F. Ellenberger's *The Discovery of the Unconscious: The History and Evolution of Dynamic Psychiatry,*[57] and Theodore Schwenk's *Sensitive Chaos,*[58] which contained drawings of our physical connection with nature. We share genes with everything that is alive, even plants.

Even though I learned that Shlain's book included many untruths, at that time I was fascinated by his addressing the chief characteristics of each hemisphere: left—doing, words, abstraction, number; right—being, images, metaphor, music.

I later learned that Robert Sapolsky's response to Gleick's book, was awareness of the pathological field of psychology. I also learned a lot from Ellenberger's book. It included knowledge of Pierre Janet's work. As said previously, Janet coined the words, *dissociation* and *subconscious,* and the first theorist, over a century ago, to know there is a connection between events in the subject's past and his or her present-day symptoms. A major insight was evoked by Ellenberger's writing—Freud and Jung's ego concept of consciousness is invalid—the ego is simply a story about one's self adopted and believed.

That fourteen-page writing preceded my definition regarding the multidimensional reflective human. Those pages were an answer to that ongoing subconscious query about a higher plane of existence.

Another event brought on positive change. The move to Poland, together with Ellenberger's book, freed me from enmeshment with any of the pathological field of psychology. I realized that psychology is similar to religion with the numerous denominations based on belief. It obviously became much easier for me to see the big picture—holistic view—from the distance of time and/or space than to distinguish what is near. Another example of an old saying worth repeating, one cannot see the forest for the trees.

* * *

Like that insight of the intertwining of my music with my writing, I have also realized that positive insights in the past are also intertwined with positive events in the present, for they, like negative events, remain in the subconscious mind and affect one's behavior.

A year after my brother's death, I moved from Maitland to Tallahassee, where my daughter and 10 month old grandson lived. That move also freed me from enmeshment in my family of origin and some truly pathological so-called friends. In contrast, my closest friends have remained in my life. With that distance of time and space they have become even more significant, for they are also creative and free from human constructionism. The creativity of a true friend was evidenced in a book she sent to me. On the dedication page she added a note, "To my darling Frances, I owe you my life. I love you without limits."

She has also expressed gratitude for knowledge of my care regarding a physical disability—scoliosis—the curvature and twisting of my spine, which resulted in numerous herniated disks. An extraordinary female chiropractor had revealed the cause: a damaged psoas muscle on the left side of my body. That muscle connects the hip to the rib cage and enables walking. I realized the source of that damage was by an incapable physician via exploratory surgery at age 24. Back pain began after that surgery.

In 2002 I was told that I would be in a wheelchair within a few years. That did not happen, for I had found corrective exercises on the internet and an excellent massage therapist. My intuitive massage therapist is, like those chaos scientists, aware of scaling systems in the body, e.g., the feet duplicate the spine and connect with numerous internal organs—the purpose of reflexology. Her healing work, together with my exercise and self-care, is gradually straightening my spine.

After a life-threatening experience with a doctor in Tallahassee, I found it unwise to trust anyone who exhibits complacency—the belief that there is no problem—or lacks humane values. I have removed all of those half-brain people from my life.

As said in the first sentence of Chapter One, my life has changed. Who I am now barely resembles the person I was 40 years ago when I lacked a sense of self-worth, perceived myself as ugly, and was emotionally dependent. My emergent mind—ongoing evolution of consciousness—definitely did contribute to knowledge of the ascending power within, especially reverence for life, which requires care for one's body.

Recently, my trustworthy and empathic physician, who relieves my pain with medication, told me that my body is as healthy as my mind. He admires my book writing and my music.

* * *

In a sense I am still a mental health counsellor in my writing. A few people who have read my previous writings told me that it had a positive effect on their lives, including my massage therapist, who, like me, has overcome a difficult past. Two of those books contain many of the shared discoveries in this writing. Now I know that helping clients to overcome the abuse and oppression of their lives is actually personal growth and development. Had all the research knowledge shared in this book been available to me in my education, it would have contributed, many years ago, to consciousness, as well as a sense of peace, joy, and harmony. I have, indeed, achieved my life's purpose, and, hopefully, will eventually be heard.

A holistic view of mental dysfunction is that symptoms are the result of post-traumatic stress and/or dissociative disorder. "Dissociation is any of a wide array of experiences from mild detachment from immediate surroundings to more severe detachment from physical and emotional experience. The major characteristic of all dissociative phenomena involves a detachment from reality, rather than a loss of reality as in psychosis."[59] Psychosis occurs when the sequential left brain's reality is rendered unconscious; as said before, it occurs after long term and intense abuse. That experience evokes the highest realm of fear; it is the reason that the medical treatment is strong anti-anxiety medication, which has horrendous side effects.

That detachment from reality is lack of awareness of subconscious memories that continue to affect one's life in multiple dimensions—the sequential left brain, the body, and behavioral energy. That detachment can also cause unconsciousness of the higher spatial brain knowledge, including spirituality.

Initial recommendations for positive change for one's mind and life became available in my work as group counsellor at the Center for Drug Free Living. As said in Chapter Three, each session began with body stretches and relaxation. Self-knowledge began with a brief writing of personal history, as well as journaling and drawings. Knowledge of the human spirit helped them to achieve a sense of self-worth.

Each of those recommendations can be significantly advanced by the knowledge shared in this book, especially the need for introspection and kindness. My composition teacher was a person to exhibit that kindness. In a sense, he was more of a healing therapist than anyone I knew in the field of psychology. He was interested in the emotions that were expressed in my music and always listened, with non-judgmental compassion, when I shared the events that aroused those emotions.

Ideally, revolutionized psychology, based on science accomplished by men of wisdom referred to in this document, would replace the pathological field of psychology in university educational programs. It would also be necessary to promote mental health of the students who intend to be counsellors.

* * *

The 4th Movement of my Concerto is *Transitions in Space and Time, the Ascending Power Within.* When I began to write those sounds in my mind in 1915, they seemed extraordinarily familiar. Out of curiosity, I dug through my stack of discarded compositions and discovered that it had already essentially been written seventeen years before in two separate songs.

The second part of the song was originally titled *Death of Narcissus,* an ancient metaphor symbolic of words of wisdom: self-love—that narcissistic left brain ego—must die in order for humanity to flower. I only added the flowering part, the ending of that song.

The first part was originally titled *Colors.* It was a song I wrote while working at the Center for Drug Free Living. Another dimension of my sense of purpose—to promote personal growth and development—manifested in my own flowering, bringing to actual my whole self.

My fourth Concerto is essentially a story of my transitions after my awakening. Listening to the corrected and fully orchestrated composition I realized that the piano chords at the ending of the song are symbolic of the awakening vision, for those chords turn inside out and upside down to ascend to the highest point.

CHAPTER SIX

THE PATHOLOGICAL FIELD OF PSYCHOLOGY/PSYCHIATRY

There had been many encounters with the pathology of psychology. Like my own process of self-discovery, those encounters, singularly, did not have nearly the impact that the whole picture evokes. Like Sapolsky, my top-down view exposed the horrors imposed on humans in the history of psychology/psychiatry: lobotomies on thousands of people, and electric-shock therapy; the use of LSD and other inhumane experiments. Then there is the belief that behavior is primarily genetic used by many cognitive (information processing) half-brain therapists.

A subdivision of cognitive psychology—evolutionary psychology—is based on Darwin's theory of biological evolution. It is purported to be an attempt to unify psychology. It is a concept that is truly shallow and spiritless revealing that egoists abound in the field. One particularly, Harvard Professor Steven Pinker, a specialist in language and cognition, is alleged to be one of the greatest *thinkers* of our time by other half brain Flatlanders.

I was initially attracted to Pinker's work by the title of his book, *How the Mind Works.*[60] As it turned out, his writing was also a subjective confession. His is a mechanistic computational model of the functions of the brain. His mind-as-computer representation, supportive of man-as-machine, is based on genetic programming of human behavior by natural selection. That mechanistic view suggests that we, as humans, are essentially problem solvers. His science, in that book, is limited to a treatise on the functions of the human eye, what he terms "reverse engineering." I have little doubt that his detailed anatomy and functions of the human eye is indicative of his lack of visual-spatial skills.

Pinker also purports dreams to simply be screen savers of our mechanical minds. Other major issues in his book are his argument for atheism and the "selfish gene." The selfish gene was his way of expressing the predominantly gene-centered view of mental functioning—one of those mindless physical forces to which Roger Wolcott Sperry was referring.

Another of Harvard's faculty adheres to genetic trait theories: Martha Stout. Her conclusions, evidenced in her book, *The Paranoia Switch*,[61] are just as ludicrous as Pinker's when she states that even political leanings—conservative or liberal—are partly "born in the blood." Stout relies on data acquired by a 2005 research questionnaire prepared by political scientists. She also relies heavily on that myth that the world is comprised of opposites when she asserts that liberals and conservatives are necessary and a part of nature. Her ignorance is an example of the unidimensional focus of our educational systems supporting that big divide and devaluing the spatial brain's abilities.

I did not waste money or time on Pinker's subsequent books after discovering how his mind works. Relying on synopses of his writings,

Pinker appears to continue his rhetoric when he promotes language as a reflection of the user's nature, disregarding the influence of the cultural language of his/her environment. It reminds me of a culturally prejudiced ignorant client at the drug treatment center who said, "I know that I would speak English no matter where I was born."

I wondered what Pinker would say about those *idiot savants,* intellectually challenged, especially regarding language, who evidence phenomenal spatial abilities. He ignores the fact that a child's initial sequential learning is acquired by modeling. Another basic reality—without stimulation and human touch, an infant's brain does not develop and frequently death occurs.

Richard Dawkins is another unbalanced so-called scientist with a massive ego. He, too, perpetuates the gene centered view of human thought, emotion, and behavior. While many of his rational, bottom-up conclusions regarding religion in *The God Delusion,*[62] are agreeable, his insight, like Pinker's, is impaired by lack of spatial brain development.

Betty Edwards was generous when she said, "Half a brain is better than none; a whole brain would be better."[63] As those ancient sages knew, extremist ego centered people bring increase to no one but themselves. Both Dawkins and Pinker contribute to our spiritless world by supporting "Darwinian inequities,"[64] which results in classification of people and a materialistic and fractious society.

Then there is the human designed statistical research, like those political scientists concluding that political preferences are "born in the blood." A conclusion which has nothing to do with science or truth. In my own study of statistical proof, it became evident that the experimental design can be manipulated to gain the desired result by choosing the factors that would prove their point and omitting the factors that would not. Many of those results comprise the arbitrary divisions that do abound like William Herbert Sheldon's body types and personality, Paul D. MacLean's triune brain, Howard Gardner's nine different kinds of intelligence, to name only a few.

I had become fascinated with the human brain in undergraduate school and took extracurricular courses in physiology, reflecting the many dimensions within the body, especially the chemical and electrical interplays within a single neuron in the brain. It was limited, though, by what Sperry called the "reductionism to the atomic level." Nothing was found regarding what I was really searching for, knowledge regarding dreams. The only references to dreams and dreaming in my education were Carl Jung's symbols and Freud's assertion that dreams are simply wish fulfillment.

The major focus of my two-year master's degree was on diagnosis, which included memorizing the DSM—*Diagnostic and Statistical Manual of Mental Disorders.* That psychological bible is in opposition to any ethical code. Labeling a person is dehumanizing to the person labeled as well as to the labeler. It narrows one's perception of the other, and it becomes practically impossible to actually see the whole person.

Research revealed that the first DSM, published in 1952, attracted controversy and criticism from countless professionals, many who asserted that it is unscientific and formed by the beliefs of a few powerful psychiatrists. Its publication was financially backed by drug companies. Put simply, those powerful psychiatrists and the drug companies are in the helping profession for the money. The DSM does reveal some valid behavioral patterns, yet it identifies the symptoms as the disease. The consequence is the overuse of medications, with detrimental side effects, to treat the symptoms.

One modern person who approached wholeness was Systems Theorist Murray Bowen, well-known by family therapists, yet his work was also ignored in my education. As said before, Bowen used degrees of differentiation as a measure of mental health in order to achieve individuation as one matures. Essentially, it is abstracting oneself from an enmeshed family. As said in Chapter Four regarding a man of wisdom, Humanist Psychologist Abraham Maslow, was only mentioned in reference to Psychologist Carl Rogers.

Another find regarding counseling was *Persuasion and Healing*[65] by Jerome Frank, PhD, M.D. (co-authored with his daughter) published in 1991. Frank suggests that the theories actually do not seem to matter in the therapeutic process. His 20-year endeavor to determine the outcome across a broad spectrum of theoretical models resulted in his conclusion: "It is not the mastery of technique or the belief system of a therapist that accounts for positive change, but rather his or her personal qualities" (the person). He also asserts many therapies are surprisingly similar to rhetoric (persuasion) and hermeneutics (interpretation).

The title of his book, *Persuasion and Healing,* provides a clue to the responses in his study. The words, *rhetoric* and *hermeneutics,* cannot be linked with healing. His conclusion is agreeable—the *person* of the therapist can support positive change; he is wrong regarding beliefs, for belief and behavior are inseparable—the continuum that comprises that person. As is the case with most so-called research, the results are dubious. How can one distinguish if actual healing occurs or the subjects have simply learned the psychobabble and been persuaded to comply with the therapist's rhetoric? Another example of enmeshment. Regarding hermeneutics (interpretation)—anyone who interprets the symbols of another or knows what is in their mind is, like Freud, engaged in projection—assigning to others what is in one's own mind.

If one even began to document the damage imposed by psychiatrists, psychologists, counselors, and psychotherapists with their rhetoric and hermeneutics, it would fill countless volumes, and in fact, it does. Phyllis Chesler's *Women and Madness*[66] was the first one found. It exposes the horrors—labels, hospitalization, over-medication, rape...—imposed on women by sexist therapists and psychiatrists.

There are now, and have been, numerous fads adopted by psychologists. Some of those fads are so mind intrusive they qualify as criminal. The famous case of Sybil with multiple personalities has been proven to be a hoax. *Sybil Exposed: Memory, Lies and Therapy*[67] by Journalist Debbie Nathan, is precise in the title of her commentary, which also addresses the [false] recovered memory debacle. That hoax has also been described as a cult-like entrapment, and in *Remembering Trauma,* as a "disgraceful therapeutic craze."[68] It was a craze that turned into a witch hunt destroying countless lives. What made it even more evil is that it was a craze that brings into question the innumerable valid cases of sexual abuse tucked away by silence.

Therapists also use persuasive tactics, false interpretation, and the power of suggestion during hypnotic trance to achieve past life regression memories. One cannot become more distanced from the past than to place the source of difficulties in another life. The use of hypnotic trance, in any case, is dangerous, for it increases the power of the psycho-therapist over the mind of another.

Another fad that toys with the mind is Neuro-linguistic programming, which has nothing to do with neuroscience. Its use—to gain control over a client—is as dangerous as Richard Bandler, one of its founders, a murderer and cocaine trafficker.[69] Similar is the relatively new pop psychology Eye Movement Desensitization Processing that has proven to be about as affective as faith healing, which is even less effective than cognitive therapy. Cognitive therapy, at its best, is nothing more than crisis intervention.

I was unaware of conservative Christian Psychologist James Dobson's 1977 book, *Dare to Discipline,* until the results of his promotion of corporal punishment reached the media: the suffering and death of children, even infants, at the hands of their caretakers. That Dobson's brutality is lauded and taught is horrifying.

Less dangerous is the fad of Transactional Analysis—an extension of Freudian concepts—with a focus on conscious conversations. A book on that subject is *TA Today,*[70] coauthored by Ian Stewart and Christian Psychologist Vann Joines. It includes some mindless concepts: there is no such thing as a victim; the assertion that clients made decisions in infancy, and, as children, planned their whole lives.

Then there is rebirthing, the child within, forgiveness, gurus, inspirational speakers, life coaching, spiritualist (psychic) advisors, and those whose rhetoric includes their religious beliefs. Not a complete listing; the current popularized label seems to be bi-polar disorder—perhaps symbolic of our humanly constructed unbalanced world.

Reforming or transforming the system as a whole is prevented by the system itself—the self-governing, belief-based entity—a closed system. While one might argue that the variety of concepts is reflective of an open system, it is not. Instead it is an indication of psychology's deterioration toward entropy—a measure of how disorganized a system is—reflective of our closed human systems at large. Just as our predominately sequential world exhibits structural violence, so does psychology. Even though it has a code of ethics that speaks of human values, it lacks humane values in practice.

It is a system that protects the therapists who practice those dangerous fads, condoning, as well, the continual teaching of fads in required Continuing Education courses. I found out that it protects the even more dangerous practitioner, like my evil therapist, for I filed a complaint against him during the writing of my first book, and it had no result. Then there are those dangerous practitioners who use drugs to conveniently alter the minds of our most vulnerable population—children and the elderly. There are proven humanistic alternatives to the use of drugs, especially with children, e.g. Howard Glasser's *The Nurtured Heart Approach*,[71] which is essentially healthy parenting training.

Perhaps by being intertwined with the drug companies, through their generous financial support, the American Psychiatric Association and American Medical Association have, as well, obstructed valid research regarding the long-term effect of massive doses of inoculations on brain development.

I discovered that it is equally important to focus on that which is missing. There was nothing in my education even approaching neuroscience much less the effect of violence on the human brain.

There was not a single word about our dual hemispheres or the human spirit. There was no definitive statement of mental health.

Throughout my training in the actual practice of counseling, there was not a single time that client's dreams were included, even though it is a fact that almost every human dreams, whether recalled or not. As said previously, the only exception are those people whose parietal lobe, behind the frontal lobes, has been damaged by stroke. In other words, there was no science at all in any of my education in psychology.

Also missing was a single therapeutic intervention which included grief, despite the distinguished work of Swiss Psychiatrist Elisabeth Kubler-Ross, made accessible in her 1969 book *On Death and Dying.* Those stages of grief are everywhere: denial, bargaining, anger, sadness; by no means a complete list, but those most obvious. Resolution, the closure attained through the grief process is when one learns to let go of the past. Not only was grief ignored but many interventions discouraged grief with the excuse that people get stuck in it. It is an idea that discounts the fact that denial is also a stage of grief and can be readily identified in unbalanced people.

It is not a joke—the use of the term *psycho* therapist—that many practitioners are as unbalanced as the patients they treat, obvious in their subjective confessions. Like the Jewish female counselor I had the misfortune of encountering who believes "People do not change." She took pride in having destroyed the life of a university professor with gossip about his extra-marital affairs (with her). Her children, as well, evidenced extreme lack of balance.

A Wicca psychologist surprised me with her statement that "Everything is symbols;" it is, for those who are semi-conscious, lacking in introspection and self-knowledge. I was shaken by a cognitive (information processing) counselor who was untouched by the tragedy of violence in her client's lives; lack of compassion was obvious with her assertion that she was an objective counselor.

A major disappointment was over a Self-Psychology supervisor from whom I sought support for my work and to learn more about advances in dynamic psychology. In a social situation he bragged about having had sex with his client because "Women are seductive." Then there are those extremists regarding self-esteem who preach self-love—that narcissistic massive ego which sublimates the spatial brain capacity. The list goes on and on and on.

Another April, 1990 poem was applicable to two encounters with complacent professionals working in the field:

Do not bother with those who do not seek,
hiding behind the scene of perfection;
their pointing fingers show
the wrong direction.

One was an experience with my psychoanalytic professor in graduate school, one of the "comfortable white males" referred to by Gould. He is Freudian, Christian, with the accompanying massive ego. One day in the lecture room I asked a question regarding inconsistencies between theorists and methods of treatment; he walked to my chair in the classroom, stood over me with a threatening posture, grimaced face, and attacked me verbally. I sat there as though frozen until I heard a fellow student say, "How can you sit there and let him talk to you like that?"

There was little difference between that professor and a rigid behaviorist psychologist, a so-called expert in psychological testing. During a job interview, my initial encounter with him, his arrogance and meanness, evidenced in hostile closed questions, was dumbfounding. I chose not to pursue any role that would bring me into any further contact. It was not surprising but deeply saddening to learn, a few years later, that his teenage son committed suicide. The sadness was for the depth of despair that young man had suffered.

Another psychoanalytic professor was a ridiculous, egoistic believer in reincarnation. In her private practice she used hypnosis for the client to recall what had happened in a previous life that was causing disturbance in the present. One time I had a client who had been to her. It turned out that the professor, through hypnotic suggestion, convinced her that an abuse was in a previous life. It was a memory of rape in her teenage years, which had become subconscious due to a sense of guilt and silence.

As in all professions and belief systems, including religion, I know there are individuals in the counseling field who exhibit the crucial elements of insight and intuition who can provoke positive change in their work. I had the good fortune of meeting only a few, some who use art and music therapy for self-expression, as well as a child therapist who advocated parenting training. There was a time when I envisioned working toward unifying psychological theories. I knew from the moment of my awakening in 1991, the need for a revolution.

The current field of psychology, by ignoring science, particularly neuroscience, continues to be dominated by the sequential world of measurement—treating people as objects—as well as that gene centered view; both have obstructed consciousness. There are psychologists and so-called social scientists who find value in the *Book of Changes*, beginning with Wilhelm's friend, Carl Jung, who wrote the Forward to Wilhelm's editions.

It is obvious to me now that the distorted *Book of Changes* and the concepts of Yang (male) and Yin (female) had an influence on Carl Jung's theories, confirming his religious background and that patriarchal view; it is evidenced in his words, "But no one can evade the fact, that in taking up a masculine calling, studying, and working in a man's way, woman is doing something not wholly in agreement with, if not directly injurious to, her feminine nature."[72] He progressed, however, in his theory of the anima and animus as archetypes and elements of the collective unconscious. "The unconscious of a man includes the feminine personality; the unconscious of a woman includes the masculine personality."[73]

As to Jung's collective unconscious concept—it simply is not true. The only things that are collective is the fact that we are all a part of nature, reflected in the multidimensional human; it is also the same spirit that exists in each of us. His concept of the unconscious is called shadow. Essentially it is subconscious that does bring shadow to one's life; he said that children's conscious problems are a result of "the evil within oneself as well as outside."[74]

Freud's concept of the unconscious is the id, which is obviously human instincts. Instincts were given credence by Sperry. He also addressed Freud's id as being "full of carnal impulses and a predisposition to Oedipal and other complexes."[75]

Personally offensive are those psychiatrists and psychologists who associate creativity with mental illness. One of those psychiatrists founded "Creativity and Madness," a Continuing Education Course purported to be psychological studies of art and artists, famous creative people from the past. It is the subjective material novels and movies are made of. It is lunacy to believe one can interpret the symbols in artists' or musicians' creative work.

As I have experienced, interpreting my own symbols expressed in my poetry, art, and music required extensive introspection to achieve self-knowledge. No one can possibly know what is in the mind of another multidimensional human, for in addition to space-time-matter-energy are the countless environmental differences unique to each individual. No biography can cover all of the variables that affect thought, emotion, and behavior or the complexities of survival.

* * *

The pathological field of psychology was validated in the 2011, *Zeitgeist, Moving Forward* documentary. The connection between violence and mental illness is addressed by Gaber Mate', M.D., one of the spokesmen in that film; he specializes in addictive disorders. His statement, "Blaming genes is a cop-out that allows people to ignore the societal factors that contribute to violence."

Another significant spokesman in that film is James Gilligan, a Psychologist who works with imprisoned people who have committed violent crimes. Gilligan reports that those criminals are victims of incredible violence—victims who become perpetrators. He also states that we "can't understand anything outside its environment." That is true, however, he lacks awareness of the multiple dimensions that are at the root of crime, including jealousy, hatred, misogyny....., and even materialism.

Richard Wilkinson, a British social epidemiologist and another spokesman is obviously aware of neuroplasticity, for in that documentary he addresses the biological effect of violence. He proposes that it can even activate genes. It is doubtful that is true, and he does not even address the fact that emotional and psychological abuse can be just as damaging.

As said in Chapter Three, Stanford neurobiologist Robert Sapolsky also appeared in that film. He knows that behavior is not genetic, and that stress plays a major role.

The results of stress were also addressed by Mate' who introduced the terms e*xplicit* and *implicit* memories. Obviously unaware of the attributes of the sequential and spatial hemispheres, he asserts that implicit memories sustain addiction—those authentic emotions that have been rendered unconscious. Another example he presents regards adopted infants who felt the pain of being taken away from their mothers. Mate' is also aware that without human touch, infants' brains do not develop.

Essentially, the psychological aspect of that film gives credence to the sequential hemisphere-spatial hemisphere-body-behavior continuum; damage to any dimension affects the others.

Structural violence was also a focus in *Zeitgeist, Moving Forward;* numerous examples were given linking that violence to the profiteers—the product of social constructionism—the materialism that has taken over much of the human world. A world where even illness, physical and mental, is advanced for profit.

The solution to resolve the problems of our shallow and violent world contained a concept that is most agreeable, the need for a revolution and a restructuring of society more in tune with nature, one founded in a resource-based economy. It would dissipate the inherent depravity in capitalism, which fosters economic inequality, and replacing it with a social system that meets changeless human needs.

That restructuring of society's educational systems, should, as said in Chapter Five, replace the pathological field of psychology with revolutionized psychology, based on the science of the men of wisdom acknowledged in this document. That positive change, especially wholeness and humane values, could become a pervasive influence on the world by replacing the materialism influenced by the flatland field of psychology.

EPILOGUE

While it has not been recommended to use the distorted *I Ching, Book of Changes,* I sometimes use it to gain a holistic view of my detailed writing. Of course, I override the distortions, especially the evil female oppression. While I am not in sync with a book, I am with the underlying principles of nature.

After completion of this book, my synchronicity with the *I Ching was* obvious when the hexagram obtained was #27—*Providing Nourishment*—my sense of purpose. Also obtained was the ruler of the hexagram, the nine at the top: "The source of nourishment. Awareness of danger brings good fortune." The descriptive comment included, "This describes a sage of the highest order, from whom emanate all influences that provide nourishment for others."

After editing and making corrections I obtained hexagram #26— *The Taming Power of the Great,* as well as the nine at the top: "One obtains the way to heaven. Truth works in the great." The comment includes, "honored as a sage and is nourished." It validated my insight that by providing nourishment for others, one's self is nourished.

While I am definitely modest, my spirituality and sense of self-worth has developed immensely to achieve the celestial region of my mind.

Since this is my final writing, I am hopeful that I can compose more music reflecting the beauty and harmony of nature, the phenomenon of being, as well as the gift of life.

APPENDIX I

A PSALM OF WISDOM

Do not say with sad expression
Life is but an empty dream!
When the spatial brain is suppressed
Things are not what they seem.

Life is real! Life is earnest!
And wholeness should be its goal:
The self's multiple dimensions
United by the empowered soul.

Not enjoyment and not sorrow
Is our destined end or way,
But to act, that each tomorrow
Find us further than today.

Art is long, and time is fleeting;
Our creative and timely minds
Must face the reality of death
And the value of time.

In the reality of the bitter-sweet
And the complexities of life,
Be not oppressed by myth beliefs
Be a hero in the strife.

Trust no future, however pleasant!
Grieve the past and rise about it.
Act, act in the living present,
Empowered by the soul's cosmic spirit.

Lives of great men all remind us
We can achieve a utopian mind,
And departing, leave behind us
Footprints on the sands of time.

Footprints that perhaps another,
Lacking in self-knowledge,
A forlorn sister or brother
Seeing, shall take heart again.

Let us then, be up and doing,
With fortitude for any fate,
Still achieving, still pursuing;
For insights we must learn to wait.

APPENDIX II

AUDITORY-SEQUENTIAL AND VISUAL-SPATIAL LEARNING[76]

The Auditory-Sequential Learner	The Visual-Spatial Learner
Thinks primarily in words	Thinks primarily in pictures
Has auditory strengths	Has visual strengths
Relates well to time	Relates well to space
Is a step-by-step learner	Is a whole-part learner
Learns by trial and error	Learns concepts all at once
Progresses sequentially from easy to difficult material	Learns complex concepts easily; Struggles with easy skills
Is an analytical thinker	Is a good synthesizer
Attends well to details	Sees the big picture; may miss details
Follows oral directions well	Reads maps well
Does well at arithmetic	Is better at math reasoning than computation
Learns phonics easily	Learns whole words easily
Can sound out spelling words	Must visualize words to spell them
Can write quickly and neatly	Much better at keyboarding than handwriting
Is well organized	Creates unique methods of organization

Can show steps of work easily	Arrives at correct solutions intuitively
Excels at rote memorization	Learns best by seeing relationships
Has good auditory short-term memory	Has good long-term visual memory
May need some repetition to reinforce learning	Learns concepts permanently; does not learn by drill and repetition
Learns well from instructions	Develops own methods of problem solving
Learns in spite of emotional reactions	Is very sensitive to teachers' attitudes
Is comfortable with one right answer	Generates unusual solutions to problems
Develops fairly evenly	Develops quite asynchronously (unevenly)
Usually maintains high grades	May have very uneven grades
Enjoys algebra and chemistry	Enjoys geometry and physics
Masters other languages in classes	Masters other languages through immersion
Is academically talented	Is creatively, technologically, mechanically, emotionally or spiritually gifted
Is an early bloomer	Is a late bloomer

APPENDIX III

A WRITING BY CHARLES ANDY WALL

I believe that 18 days from today I'll be released from jail. I believe I shouldn't be here for getting drunk and being an alcoholic, but I'm here.

I think that's my only negative statement of this letter. The purpose of my writing is to tell you of the faith I've gradually found in 41 years of living. Faith in God, I know is a matter of attitude in looking for the beauty to be seen in living day by day. Believe me, it takes practicing a good attitude to see beauty sitting behind bars looking at pea-green walls.

I have pictures I've torn from magazines and tooth-pasted up in front of my steel leaf desk sticking out from the wall. One is a pair of wood ducks whose beauty needs no explanation. Another picture has a cat snuggling up to a fox that has been blinded by a car running over her. The next has a big black circus bear sitting with a little boy looking over his shoulder at Thomas the Tank Engine and Friends magazine. Another picture shows a fox trying with all his might to push an old fat goose in a baby carriage.

None of these pictures show fear or anger, only mutual respect for life and unselfish love. That love is the essence of my faith in God.

I was told as a child in Sunday school that God is love and he lives in the hearts of men everywhere. I believe that.

I have a picture of a little girl, barefooted, on crutches, leaning back on a stone wall that reminds me never to feel sorry for myself. And when I look close at the pain and heartache in her little face, I can't help but shed a tear. For the gift God gave me to feel unselfish love and compassion, I am eternally grateful.

To the powerful faith I see in my picture of three polar bears swimming out to sea with not even an iceberg in sight, I will forever cling to. What I believe is that there's something good and beautiful in everything I see if I look for it. God made it that way.

Then I look at the picture of a guillotine and wonder why, oh why must men conjure up ways to hurt each other instead of turning in to the beauty God made for us?

Bob Dylan sang the answer about the same time I graduated from high school. "The answer my friend, is blowin' in the wind."

A POEM OF STEPHEN HAWKING'S LIFE REFLECTIVE OF LONGFELLOW'S POETIC WISDOM

Stephen Hawking did not say in
Mournful numbers life is but an empty
Dream. He gave credence to the spirit,
The cosmic life force, the unifying and
Ascending force in nature and humans.

He knew that life is real and life is earnest
And the grave is not its goal.
Through his own field of battle with
His physical matter, his fortitude
And reverence for life was remarkable.

Fortitude was founded in love for his wife
And encouraged by Wagner's classical music which
Told stories, especially of the brave dealing with
The complexities of survival. His synchronicity
With nature awakened his spiritual mind.

It is highly likely that the energy evidenced
In string theory is the light of the spirit, for it
Exists in all life, the fifth dimension of humans
As Hawking said, the same spirit exists
In all of us, and is underlying all life.

Regardless of his physical handicap,
His brilliant mind was free, especially from
The herd of humans, driven by belief in a
Ridiculous controlling god, who view life as
A way station and oppressing the spirit.

Stephen Hawking was a true hero and
A great man, fostering what is right and good;
Reminding others that life can be sublime
By achieving self-actualization and
The celestial region of the mind.

Through introspection he knew that
Enjoyment or sorrow was not his
Destined end or way, but to act so
Each tomorrow would find him further
Than each gift of today.

Even though his body died, he has left eternal
Footprints on the sands of time; footprints
That can encourage others to achieve the human
Potential for wholeness: space-time-matter-energy
Reflective of the wisdom of nature.

He was up and doing with the inner strength
To deal with any fate, delving to the depth and
The height of life, still pursuing, still achieving
Insight regarding nature's laws, achieved by
His whole mind empowered by cosmic energy.

ENDNOTES

Chapter One

1 The free dictionary.com

2 Wikipedia

3 Sperry, Roger W., *Mind, Brain, and Humanist Values, U.* Chicago Press, 1965. This Article can be found at http://people, uncw.edu/Puente/sperry/sperrypaters/60s/125-1966.pdf.lv Wikipedia

4 www.merriam-webster.com/dictionary/complacency.

5 Edwards, Betty. *Drawing on the Right Side of the Brain*, Jeremy P. Tarcher/Putnam, 1989 An expanded and updated edition was published in 1999: *The New Drawing on the Right Side of the Brain*, is a product of Betty Edwards' evolving thought.

6 Sullivan, Harry Stack, M.D., *The Interpersonal Theory of Psychology,* W. W. Norton & Company, 1953

7 Gould, Stephen Jay, *The Mismeasure of Man*, W. W. Norton & Co., 1981

8 Szasz, Thomas S., M.D., *The Myth of Mental Illness, Foundations of a Theory of Personal Conduct*, Harper and Row, 1974

9 Ellenberger, Henri F., *The Discovery of the Unconscious: The History and Evolution of Dynamic Psychiatry,* Basic Books, 1970

10 Shlain, Leonard, *Art & Physics: Parallel Visions in Space, Time, & Light,* William Morrow Company, Inc., 1991

11 Anthony Storr, *The Essential Jung.* Princeton University Press, 1983

[12] https://en.wikipedia.orgwiki/Gottfried_Wilhelm_Leibnix

[13] www.enwikipedia.org/wiki/Self-fulfilling_prophecy

[14] Gleick, James, *Chaos: Making a New Science*, Penguin Books, 1988

Chapter Two

[15] Hawking, Stephen, *A Brief History of Time*, Bantam Books, 1990

[16] *New York Times,* Nov. 9, 1930

[17] Capra, Fritjof, *The Science of Leonardo: Inside the Mind of the Great Genius of the Renaissance,* Double Day, 2007

[18] http://www.thefreedictionary.com/continuum

[19] http://thinkexist.com/quotes/albert_einstein/

[20] *The I Ching or Book of Changes*, The Richard Wilhelm Translation rendered into English by Cary F. Baynes, Princeton University Press, 1997, Page 505

[21] Brabezon, James, *Albert Schweitzer: A Biography*, G. P. Putnam's Sons, 1975

[22] www.merriam-webster.com/dictionary/fortitude

[23] Voneida, Theodore J., *A Biographical Memoir*, National Academies Press, 1997, available at www.nasonline.org

[24] http://www. En.wikipedia.org/wiki/Roger_Wolcott_Sperry

[25] https://en.wikipedia.org/wiki/Activity-dependent_plasticity

[26] Sperry, Roger W., *Holding Course Amid Shifting Paradigms,* From proof for The Metaphysical Foundation of Modern Science: Issues of Causality. Eds. W. Harman and J. Clark, Institute of Noetic Sciences (in press, 1994) This Article can be found at: people.uncw.edu/puentel/sperry/papers/1994 (#282)

[27] Voneida, Theodore J., *Roger Wolcott Sperry*, The National Academies Press, found at website: http://www.nap.edu/html/biomems/rsperry.html

28 *Mind, Brain, and Humanist Values,* Roger W. Sperry. From *New Views of the Nature of Man,* John R. Platt (Ee.). Chicago Press, 1965

29 *The I Ching or Book of Changes,* The Richard Wilhelm Translation rendered into English by Cary F. Baynes, Princetorn University Press, 1997

30 Paine, Thomas, *The Age of Reason*

31 http://en.wikipedia.org/wiki/Bertrand_Russell

32 Arcones, Pedro Ccinos, *Matriarcado en China: madres, reinas, diosas, chamanes,* Madrid, 2011

33 Huang, Alfred, *The Complete I Ching*, Inner Traditions, 1998

34 Meyer, Marvin, *The Gnostic Gospels of Jesus*, Harper Collins Publishers, 2005

Chapter Three

35 Gould, Stephen Jay, *The Mismeasure of Man*, W. W. Norton & Co., 1981

36 Kevles, Daniel J., *In the Name of Eugenics*: *Genetics and the Uses of Human Heredity*, Harvard University Press, 1995

37 Edwards, Betty. *Drawing on the Right Side of the Brain*, Jeremy P. Tarcher/Putnam, 1989

38 http://www.authorama.com/flatland-1.html

39 Ellis, Eugenia Victoria, and Reithmayr, Andrea G., *Claude Bragdon & the Beautiful Necessity,* Cary Graphic Arts Press, Rochester Institute of Technology, Rochester, New York, 2010

40 Banchoff, Thomas F., *Beyond the Third Dimension: Geometry, Computer Graphics, and Higher Dimensions,* Scientific American Library, 1990

41 Berger, Peter L., *The Sacred Canopy,* Anchor Books, 1969

42 http://dictionary,com/browse/socialconstructionism

43 Maguire, Daniel C. and Shaikh, Sa' Diyya, *Violence Against Women in Contemporary World Religions*, The Pilgrim Press, 2007

[44] Farmer, Paul, *Pathologies of Power: Health, Human Rights, and the New War on the Poor,* University of California Press, 2005

[45] Kidder, Tracy, *Mountains Beyond Mountains: The Quest of Dr. Paul Farmer, A Man Who Would Cure the World,* Random House, Inc., 2003   The quoted sentence is on the back cover of Tracy Kidder's book, a biography of Paul Farmer.

[46] Jung, Carl G., *Man and His Symbols*, Dell Publishing, 1968

[47] Brown, H. Jackson, Jr., *Life's Little Treasure Book ON WISDOM,* Rutledge Hill Press, 1994

Chapter Four

[48] www.thefreedictionary.com/insight

[49] Sommers, Christina Hoff, and Satel, Sally, M.D. *One Nation Under Therapy: How the Helping Culture is Eroding Self-reliance,* McMillian, 2006

[50] Silverman, Linda Kreger, *Upside Down Brilliance: The Visual-spatial Learner,* Denver:Deleon Publishing, 2002

[51] http://www.thefreedictionary.com/introspection

[52] Vekquin, K.M., An overview of Competing Theories of Schizophrenia, 2009, found at website: http://vekquin.com/articles/schizophrenia.html.

[53] Edwards, Betty. *Drawing on the Right Side of the Brain*, Jeremy P. Tarcher/Putnam, 1989

Chapter Five

[54] www.emedicinehealth.co

[55] Gleick, James, *Chaos*, Penguin Books, 1987

[56] Shlain, Leonard, *Art & Physics, Parallel Visions in Space, Time & Light,* William Morrow and Company, Inc., 1991

[57] Ellenberger, Henri F., *The Discovery of the Unconscious: The History and Evolution of Dynamic Psychiatry,* Basic Books, 1970

[58] Schwenk, Theodor, *Sensitive Chaos, The Creation of Flowing Forms in Water and Air*, Rudolf Steiner Press, London, 1965

[59] www.enwikipedia.org/wiki/psychology's dissociative disorder

Chapter Six

[60] Pinker, Steven, *How the Mind Works,* W. W. Norton and Co., 1997

[61] Stout, Martha, *The Paranoia Switch*, Sarah Crichton Books, 2007

[62] Dawkins, Richard, *The God Delusion,* First Mariner Books, 2008

[63] Edwards, Betty. *The New Drawing on the Right Side of the Brain*, Jeremy P. Tarcher/Putnam, 1999

[64] Ellis, Eugenia Victoria, and Reithmayr, Andrea G., *Claude Bragdon & the Beautiful Necessity,* Cary Graphic Arts Press, Rochester Institute of Technology, Rochester, New York, 2010. "Darwinian inequities" is a phrase used in Chapter 6, Architecture and the "Spirit" of Democracy, referring to the classification of people resulting in the toxins of a materialistic and fractious society.

[65] Frank, Jerome D. and Frank, Julia B., *Persuasion and Healing: A Comparative study of Psychotherapy,* John Hopkins University Press, 1991

[66] Chesler, Phyllis, *Women and Madness,* Harcourt Brace Jovanovich, 1989

[67] http://www.salon.com/2011/10/16/sybil_exposed_memory _lies_and_therapy/

[68] McHugh, Paul, Book Review, The Wall Street Journal, June 29, 2008, reviewing Richard J. McNally's Book, *Remembering Trauma*, Belknap/Harvard, 2003

[69] http://www.voxfux.com/features/cia_murder.html

[70] Stewart, Ian and Joines, Vann, *TA Today,* Lifespace Publishing, 1987

[71] Glasser, Howard, *Transforming the Difficult Child,* available on 2003 video at website, www.difficultchild.com

[72] Chesler, Phyllis, *Women and Madness,* Harcourt Brace Jovanovich, 1989

[73] wikipedia.org/wiki/Anima_and_animus

[74] Jung, Carl G., *Man and His Symbols*, Dell Publishing, 1968

[75] Sperry, Roger W., *Mind, Brain, and Humanist Values*, from Platt, John R. *New Views of the Nature of Man,* U.Chicago Press, 1965

Appendix Two

[76] http://www.education.com/reference/article/Ref_Visual_Learner/